TOGETHER

W.E

DECIDE

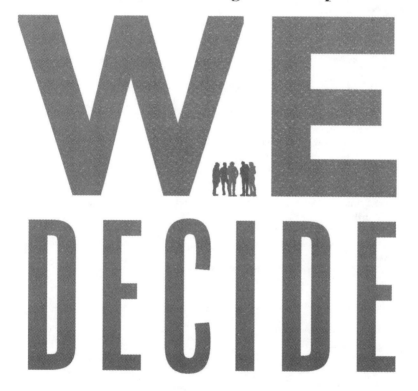

TOGETHER

An Essential Guide for Making Good Group Decisions

WE
DECIDE

CRAIG FRESHLEY

GREENLEAF
BOOK GROUP PRESS

Published by Greenleaf Book Group Press
Austin, Texas
www.gbgpress.com

Distributed by Greenleaf Book Group

For ordering information or special discounts for bulk purchases, please contact Greenleaf Book Group at PO Box 91869, Austin, TX 78709, 512.891.6100.

Design and composition by Greenleaf Book Group
Cover design by Greenleaf Book Group
Cover Images: ©iStockphoto/AlexSava, ©iStockphoto/aarrows, ©iStockphoto/eobrazy, and ©iStockphoto/Bastian Weltjen

Publisher's Cataloging-in-Publication data is available.

Print ISBN: 978-1-62634-950-6

eBook ISBN: 978-1-62634-951-3

Part of the Tree Neutral® program, which offsets the number of trees consumed in the production and printing of this book by taking proactive steps, such as planting trees in direct proportion to the number of trees used: www.treeneutral.com

TreeNeutral®

Printed in the United States of America on acid-free paper

22 23 24 25 26 27   10 9 8 7 6 5 4 3 2 1

First Edition

To my wife, Carol.
Thanks for walking with me even though I'm such a weirdo.

Contents

List of Figures

ACKNOWLEDGMENTS

LET'S START WITH a land acknowledgment. I live and work on land that is a homeland for the Wabanaki, a confederacy that once consisted of fourteen or more Indigenous tribes and several bands, and today principally consists of the Mi'kmaq, the Maliseet, the Passamaquoddy, and the Penobscot nations. This book is made from trees grown on the homelands of the Indigenous—lands taken from them. I honor with gratitude the Indigenous people before me and among me.

Second, I want to acknowledge my privileges[1] that have allowed me to become well educated, pursue my dream job, and write a book. Because I was born male and white to a middle-class American family, I have had few barriers and many breaks. Further, due to my privileges, I don't fully understand what things are really like for a lot of people out there in the world, and for many people reading this book. I hope my lessons are useful, but I don't pretend to know how they should be applied in your world, different from mine. I don't know what's right for you.

Third, I want to acknowledge the varieties of gender among us. In hypothetical stories I use the pronouns *they/them/their*

---

1 For an explanation of what it means to "check your privilege," see Ijeoma Oluo's book, *So You Want to Talk About Race.*

thus allowing the reader to imagine a person of any gender. While some readers may think of these pronouns as plural, they have been used historically to refer to individuals and are even used today to refer to a single person whose gender we don't know. For example, "Oh look, someone left their cellphone. I wonder if they will come back." When I'm telling a story of a specific person whose gender I know, I use *he, she, or they* depending on the wishes of the person I'm telling you about.

Now, let me thank some folks.

The first thank-you goes to that teacher who lit a spark in me. Professor Constance Hunting at the University of Maine taught me how to write. Early drafts of this book were reviewed by Kavana Tree Bressen and Ben Linders. They just jumped in and helped. My dear friend Jim Martin commented on an early draft and has been cheering me on, always. Jessica Dafni, Kerri Sands, Wanda McNeil, and Gretchen Jaeger each had a hand in editing. I have deep gratitude to each of you for your help along the way.

I've had three top-notch professional editors for whom I'm very grateful. Sally Garland of Greenleaf Book Group served as lead editor and nurturer and did a wonderful job of both pushing me and pulling me, and I didn't even know it was happening. Chris Benguhe gave me excellent guidance and encouragement. Judy Marchman played a key role near the end. I'm very grateful to Greenleaf Design Supervisor Chase Quarterman who did a great job with the cover and the page design. Don't you think?

Thank you to my Quaker Oversight Committee: Kristna Evans, Wendy Schlotterbeck, Tess Hartford, and Kitsie Hildebrandt. I know you're there. And much gratitude to Durham Friends.

For the knowledge in this book, I have to start with thanks to two people who taught me a lot about meeting facilitation:

Caroline Estes and Henry Bourgeois. Caroline inspired me. Henry modeled and expertly facilitated hundreds of meetings that I was in. A heartfelt thanks to my clients who let me experiment and learn. I have taken many risks with clients over the years. I'm not afraid to try things live with real stakes. I have learned so much in rooms with clients who have trusted me. And a special thanks to Two Echo Cohousing Community, my neighborhood. I signed on to this big experiment in large part to learn about group dynamics. You have not disappointed! Thank you for tolerating my antics and letting me learn with you.

The last thank-you goes to my wife, Carol Nelson. This book represents a huge amount of time away from you. Thank you for your nonjudgmental gift of time and allowing me to pursue my passion over these many years.

INTRODUCTION

Good Group Decisions Are Hard—and Worthy

HERE IN AMERICA, we love the individual achievement story. The immigrant who builds a company, the Cinderella who gets to be a princess, the street kid who makes it to professional basketball, the guy who started selling cars from his driveway and now has five dealerships with his name on them, the gal who put herself through college and is now a world-class scientist. But behind each of these stories is a group, lots of groups. There's the family, the neighborhood, the team, the school. These are all groups that helped that person achieve.

Big problems are never—and never have been—solved by individuals. Oh sure, a scientific invention or discovery here and there might seem like the magic wand that provided the perfect solution, or a single idea that got turned into a law, or a single donation that named the building. But all such discoveries, ideas, and contributions were the results of thousands of people doing thousands of things that led up to "the big thing." That's what makes the world better: lots of people doing things. Lots of groups making good decisions.

IT'S NOT US VERSUS THEM, IT'S JUST US. How about we tone down the myth of individual achievement and turn up the volume on praise for groups? I wish we would give more credit more often to teams and groups for getting stuff done and for cooking up great ideas. I want to live in a world where it's hip to be a follower, to be a supporter, to be a team player. Where it's trendy to share credit with my fellows and where it's cool to invite and welcome others into my group. I want to live in a world with more we and less me. It's not us versus them, it's just us.[2]

Yet competition is very much a part of our everyday lives. There's a hypothesis woven into the fabric of every aspect of American culture. It goes like this: Let two or more people, products, or ideas compete and this will result in what's best for the group. This hypothesis is an engine of innovation in business, in sports, in law, in health care, in schools, in families, everywhere.

Yet the hypothesis is not always right. We kid ourselves into thinking that when two competing interests "duke it out" it somehow betters the gene pool or otherwise makes us all better as a human race. In reality, the rule goes like this: Let two or more people, products, or ideas compete and this will result in what's best for the winner. I don't believe in trickle-down economics and I don't believe in trickle-down benefits from winners to losers. The hypothesis is often a myth in my opinion.

---

2   Leonard Commet Krill in person and on social media.

Competition is not de facto bad, of course. A competitive mindset can serve society extremely well especially when there's an abundance of resources. Competition has spurred magnificent human creations and inventions over the ages. Competition is a great way to generate ever higher achievements, no doubt. Yet the pendulum has swung too far. Competition has been too successful in generating know-how and technology to the point where now there is a frightening scarcity of resources.

The root of the problem is this outdated paradigm. Our country's political parties are competing with each other at the expense of the nation. World nations are competing with each other at the expense of the earth. It's not new. Civilizations have competed with each other since the dawn of history: conquering, oppressing, and building wealth at the expense of others.

Why not a different paradigm? A pendulum swing in the other way for a change? Toward collaboration. Let's work together rather than against each other. Imagine a groundswell of popularity for collaboration. Imagine companies rewarding teams rather than individuals. Imagine collaborative sports and recreational activities rising in popularity on a par with competitive sports. Imagine school children being taught and modeled collaboration and communications skills, and rewarded for team/group success rather than individual success. Imagine game shows and talent shows rewarding teams instead of individual winners and losers. Imagine people who feel marginalized by competitive environments feeling valued as collaborators. So many people in America have shut down and withdrawn from civic affairs because it's viewed as too competitive, even hostile. I have seen people withdraw from all sorts of groups and activities for fear of too much hostility. Why do we have to be so mean and so competitive with each other?

Collaborative cultures hold a place for every person to participate. No one is a loser or viewed as "less than." All have gifts to give. In collaborative cultures people work with each other for the good of the group, not against each other for entertainment or for individual gain. We should be collaborating with each other against common enemies—such as climate change or national security threats—instead of against each other in the hope that beating each other up will somehow make things better.

I have seen that when disagreements are solved by force—that is, the more powerful party says, "this is how things are gonna be"—the resolution will be short-lived. It will stay in place as long as the force can stay in place, and that's always a battle. When disagreements are resolved by compromise, the resolution may last for a while but not indefinitely. Discontent resulting from having to compromise is likely to linger and grow to the point where conflict erupts again. When disagreements are resolved because the parties have come to a peaceful understanding, the resolution is much more likely to last because the incentives for challenging it magically disappear.

MY PATH

I myself was raised with an ethic of competition, that the default objective in almost any activity was to be better than others. That made me a jerk sometimes. If I look back over my evolution as a decision maker, that realization is undeniable.

My high school was a military academy, so it naturally promoted a culture of competition between squads, platoons, companies, and battalions. We also competed individually to see who had the shiniest shoes, who ran the fastest 400 meters, who got the highest grades, who got the best girls. The idea was that competition provided inspiration for achievement and so a robust culture of competition would produce high-achieving graduates destined to lead companies, governments, nonprofits, and military units. The premise was that in a competitive environment, individual effort would be maximized and the very best of all individual efforts would prevail for the benefit of everyone. In high school I learned about how our government is based on competition between the states and the federal government; competition between the executive, legislative, and judicial branches; competition between the majority and the minority. I learned about how our economic system is based on competition between companies and how our judicial system is based on competition between plaintiffs and defendants.

I took that premise—competition is always good—off to college and applied it in student government. I competed for votes and won a seat in the student senate. I competed with my fellows for "the floor," and I argued strenuously for what I thought was right. I coerced and cajoled and manipulated relationships to improve my standing. I ran for the office of student government president and won. As president, I had to handle a lot of disputes. When two clubs were feuding over an office in the student union, my idea was to lock the leaders in a room until they reached a settlement. In another instance I said, "Let's write all the disagreements on the wall and then work through them one at a time." I have since learned that these are both terrible ways to handle disputes.

After college I started a small bike courier company and continued to perpetuate the culture of competition that I had practiced in high school, learned about in college, and was raised with. As a small business owner, I competed with other companies. I expected employees in my company to compete with each other. Since we were in the business of delivering packages, it made perfect sense for employees to be compensated based on how well they could plan their routes, how fast they could ride their bikes, and on how many packages they could deliver. I set them in competition against each other.

One day we were sitting around saying how we needed a bike stand to repair bikes. You see them in bike shops holding a bike's wheels up off the floor making it easy to change tires and adjust brakes and such. But we couldn't afford one.

We started kicking around ideas. Someone thought of hanging the bike from the ceiling with straps of webbing, the type typically used for belts and harnesses. Someone suggested adding straps to the side walls for stability. Then someone else offered the idea of quick-release buckles, and another person had the idea of adding a sliding-type buckle so the height could be adjusted. In twenty minutes, we invented the most useful, versatile, portable, bike-fixing sling-gismo in the world. Total cost: $12.35. This and other group-made solutions helped us be more efficient and save costs, and they brought us closer together. They generated enthusiasm for additional ways to make our jobs more fun and our company more profitable. Group solutions gave us a sense of purpose and belonging.

One reason I started a bike courier company was that it was a pollution-free service that replaced gas-burning vehicles. I feared for the health of the natural environment, the earth's ecosystem, and future generations of humans. And I had a strong notion that our group decision-making systems—in both the public and private sectors—were not up to task. I was also starting to see that competition in decision-making often meant that the winning people and ideas didn't always produce the best result—the most benefits for the most people. And it seemed to me that there were a lot of losers. Competition causes a lot of collateral damage. I was sure that we could do better, that there must be better ways.

I sold the company and went to graduate school to study public policy and management. I wanted to learn more about the theory of group decision-making, more about how governments work and don't work, and how best to actually make good decisions for society as a whole (not just for the winners).

I got my graduate degree and went to work for the Maine State Planning Office in Augusta. *Now,* I thought to myself, *I'm really going to participate in group decision-making for my area, with high stakes!* I was going to apply the theories I had learned for new and better ways of decision-making for the public good. But I quickly fell back into old ways. By default and unable to resist, I still saw competition as the framework for everything I did. I competed with my colleagues for status and salary. I went into meetings with the goal of getting my way. I often spoke first and loudest, talking over other people in meetings. I didn't treat women well. I carried around a sense that I knew best and if only others would take notice and do things my way, the world would be better.

One day, I was assigned to staff a new program called the Maine Commission on Community Service, part of President Bill Clinton's new AmeriCorps program that was a national system of matching volunteers with community-service projects across the country—a kind of domestic Peace Corps. Every state needed to establish one of these commissions to administer the national program.

I was joined on the commission by Bob Blakesley, a veteran bureaucrat who was approaching retirement age; he had staffed dozens of commissions, written hundreds of reports, and gave the impression of being rather set in his ways. But he had something different in mind for this project.

Bob had gone to a conference and heard a presentation by Caroline Estes, an experienced consensus decision-making professional. She had opened his eyes to a new way of making public policy decisions, and he was adamant about bringing her to facilitate the new commission's kick-off retreat. So the newly minted Maine Commission on Community Service gathered for a two-day meeting at the Sugarloaf Inn in the mountains of Maine in the fall of 1995. I was there taking notes.

Bob's plan to force this new style of consensus decision-making on the commission met with skepticism. All members were appointed by the governor. They had been around Maine politics and were savvy in the ways of majority rule decision-making, and they knew how to count votes. Caroline was able to disarm the group with her gentle style and soft words as she set everyone on notice with her erect posture and quick answers to tough questions.

She explained the basic principles of consensus-style decision-making, and commission members found them hard to argue with: All views should be heard; we should take turns talking and listen to each other with full attention; we should write down our agreements and get the words right before leaving the room. What really did the trick was when she explained that the group itself would decide its own rules for deciding things, that she wasn't forcing anything on anybody.

Before that weekend I had never experienced such a productive meeting. Caroline taught us a new way of thinking about group decisions. She taught us the steps for group decision-making and then she taught us that it's more than just the steps. She taught us about attitude. She taught us that what you feel about your cause and your group and your fellows is just as important as the steps you take. Repeatedly she referenced her belief: "We each have a piece of the truth, and we make our best decisions when we put all our pieces together."[3]

And for the most part, most of us got it. I got it, especially. You might even say that I got religion. For the first time, I understood that the attitude that each person brings to the table really matters. I came to understand that an attitude of competition is not always the best attitude if you want the most gains for the most people. I came to understand that it doesn't always have to be me against you. I saw that consensus/collaborative decision-making could be effectively applied in a traditional mainstream setting. And I watched Caroline's supreme dedication to the well-being and success of the group. She stayed up late, got up early, worked during the breaks, always processing and considering what the group needed next to make them most productive. From her I learned the notion of servant leadership.[4]

Competition had pushed me to do mean things to other people. That steadfast value—the spirit of competition—gave me permission to put others down and intentionally deceive. I began to change my values. And I tried acting on my new understandings in several ways:

I became more humble. The biggest change I made was to begin to genuinely value the opinions of my

---

3   Caroline Estes, at the kickoff meeting of the Maine Commission for Community Service, Carrabassett Valley, Maine, 1995.

4   For more on this concept, see Servant Leadership by Robert Greenleaf.

peers. I went into meetings not with the goal of wanting to get my point across but with the goal of truly wanting to understand the points of others.

I led meetings differently. I saw the value in leading as a truly neutral facilitator rather than as a self-appointed know-it-all. I learned to treat all speakers equally and react to what they said without judgment, validating each and every opinion.

I learned the value of shared ground rules. At the start of a meeting, I tried to make sure everyone understood how things would work, sometimes called meeting ground rules. Rules can help make things safer or fairer, and I wanted both safety and fairness in my groups and in my meetings.

I began sharing information. With my new attitude of wanting *us* to win rather just me winning, I became more open and transparent about sharing information.

I stopped embarrassing others. I came to see that when I intentionally embarrassed or shamed someone—when I propagated fear—that person became smaller and produced less, perhaps even came to resent the group. But when I praised someone or held them up as a good example, they produced more and gave more to the group.

I learned it's OK to change my mind. Rather than sticking to my guns on a decision even in light of new information, I learned that changing my mind to get it right for the group could actually lead to greater respect from the group.

I became a Quaker. I thought to have more spirituality in my life and a Quaker Meetinghouse happened to be near my home, so I attended a few meetings. I found a shared belief in the Quaker values of *inclusion and equity*, the notion that there is that of *God in every person*. Other Quaker values like *simplicity*, *stewardship*, and *peace* made sense to me.

WHY GOOD GROUP DECISIONS ARE IMPORTANT

I now own a consulting company where I help a wide range of clients in both the public and private sectors make good group decisions. People call me a professional meeting facilitator. Over my career I've worked with hundreds of groups in board rooms, town halls, and church basements. I have seen what works and what doesn't. I've always had a strong sense that our group decision-making systems—in both the public and private sectors—were not up to task. I have seen how competition in decision-making rarely results in the winning side providing the most benefits for the most people. It seems to me that there are often a lot of losers and that competition causes a lot of collateral damage. I am sure that we can do better, that there must be a better way.

As members of the human race, we need to learn how to make better decisions. Our survival and the survival of our children depend on it. At the macro level, we need the principles of collaboration to save our species from extinction. If we don't figure out how to make better decisions in groups, our world is in peril. Or at least our future existence is. Climate change is a huge concern of all people on earth. I believe we should treat it as a common cause, a common enemy. Slowing climate change and adapting to climate change should unite all peoples of the world. The stakes are fatally high if we don't figure out how to make good decisions at this scale.

Let's take it down a notch and talk about what's at stake as citizens of different countries and states. For a country's parliament or legislature, the stakes are mostly about future generations. State and federal politicians talk about credit or blame for short-term victories or setbacks, but these governments mainly affect what happens in future years. It is today's Americans, for instance, who are benefiting from the Clean Water Act of 1972. It's today's Mainers who are benefiting from laws our legislature passed three terms ago.

Group decisions are more easily seen and felt when the affected person is close to the decision maker. Yet the stakes are often higher and bigger when the decision maker is far away. On a global level the stakes can be really high. Decisions made by our city, state, and national governments may seem far away but have profound consequences for our future.

Most of us are part of much smaller groups closer to home. Instead of governing countries or states, we are part of a town or a neighborhood and we govern committees and families. So what's at stake for the small group, the board of directors, or the team at work that is trying to get the job done? The most common complaint about group decision-making is its inefficiency—the wasted time. It's so damn inefficient when everybody has to be involved! So many bosses watch time and money get frittered away as their people have inefficient meetings.

Regardless of what stakes might be at play in your group decision and no matter the size of your group, the value of your own time is a huge stake. Your time matters. You want your decision-making processes to be efficient.

It's like building a house. If the builders don't know what they're doing—they're using trial and error, getting things shipped at random times, and have specialists showing up at the wrong times—it results in huge inefficiencies. But there's been years of accumulated house-building science, and good builders know how to do it right. They know the order of things, the sequencing. With group decisions too, the sequencing really matters. If you pay attention to doing it right, your group decisions can be very efficient, just like building a house can be.

In this book I describe the different types of decisions that various groups make, as well as the actions and attitudes that best serve group decision-making. I talk about how to make good decisions in groups efficiently—without anger or animosity. Humans have made lots of really bad decisions that have resulted in conflict, missed opportunities, and a real threat to our sustainability as a species. Good group decisions result in greater efficiency, innovation, and productivity in part because of the enthusiasm among the members. On a personal level, participating in good group decisions brings greater peace, happiness, fulfillment, and a sense of belonging. It's time we pulled together.

YOUR TIME MATTERS. YOU WANT YOUR DECISION-MAKING PROCESSES TO BE EFFICIENT.

WHO THIS BOOK IS FOR

If you are part of any group that has meetings and makes decisions, and you are finding the decision-making process frustrating, this book is for you. If your group seems stuck perhaps you need to change something, a change in leadership or a breakthrough innovation, or a new partnership. This book can help position your group members and set you up for that breakthrough innovation or other changes that will set you on a new course.

I explain the principles of group dynamics and provide practical tools for getting along with each other and for getting decisions made swiftly for the good of the group. You don't just learn how to have great meetings. You also learn how to communicate outside of meetings, how to handle conflict, and how to feel really good about your contributions to your group and to your world.

Applying the principles of this book will give your group a chance to come up with an idea that no one individual would have thought on their own. The principles in this book are designed to spark innovation and creativity in ways that can't happen without good group dynamics. If I'm sitting all by myself in an isolated room with the door closed, I'm only going to be able to come up with an idea that's already in my head. But if I'm pushed to collaborate with my colleagues in the ways that are outlined in this book, my ideas are sure to improve due to the ideas of others.

This book is also for the person who is in a leadership role in any kind of group or is a member of a group who is frustrated with how things are going. Even if the group as a whole makes no changes whatsoever, this book is going to help *you*. It's going to help you sleep better at night. It's going to help you feel better about your contributions to the group. It's going to help you make peace with your participation in the group because you will better understand what's going on and what role to play.

The principles in this book may even help you decide to leave a group or help you decide to accept the downsides and stay anyway. The principles in this book will not only help your group, they will help you have a better relationship with the group and a better relationship with yourself because you'll have a much better understanding of how you fit in with the group—or not.

If you are a warrior to save the environment or the human race, this book is for you. When we don't make good group decisions in our families, neighborhoods, towns, states, and countries, we end up destroying our common property and killing each other. The principles in this book are about making decisions for sustainability and resilience, decisions that consider long-term and far-reaching consequences, decisions that engage all the right people. Good group decisions are good for the environment and for social justice.

If you are a manager in a large organization with group decisions to make, this book is for you. The principles in this book are designed to help your people be more efficient, get along with each other better, and enjoy their jobs. And your team will produce innovative results not previously envisioned.

IF YOU THINK YOUR PURPOSE IN LIFE IS TO SUCCEED AT THE EXPENSE OF OTHERS, THIS BOOK IS NOT FOR YOU.

Let me also say a word about who this book is *not* for. If you don't want things to be better for the group as a whole over the long term, then this book is not for you. If you think your purpose in life is to succeed at the expense of others, this book is not for you. If you think that the main purpose for joining a group is to get as much as you can from the group for free, this book is not for you. This book is not going to help you personally succeed at the expense of the group. Go read another book for that. There are lots of them. The principles and tips in this book will only work and be valuable when you want your group to succeed over the interest of individuals.

My hope is that this book will be a player in a forthcoming wave of populist support for collaboration; that collaboration becomes a thing, a really big thing, and that this book helps that. I want collaboration to become "the way to be," mainstream, and not second to competition. That collaboration will be hip. Everyone will be doing it! That group decision-making will be done a whole lot more because of this book. And that many more people will be included in group decision-making, allowing for otherwise marginalized people to have a voice.

I have tried to the best of my ability to summarize and present what I have learned in my professional career in these pages. When you are finished with this book, I hope you will be provoked and inspired to go and do group decision-making, to have the courage to lead groups or meetings, and to be a much better participant in the group processes that you are already a part of. I hope you will want to charge ahead on your own mission to make our world more collaborative and share what you've learned with other people. It's also my hope that this book fully illuminates the benefits of making decisions in groups rather than in isolation or denial. For long-term, high-stakes decisions, collaboration is hands-down the best way and so much more effective than a single leader making decisions in an office with the door closed. Group decision-making is what our world needs to solve the big problems of our world, our country, our states, our communities—even our households. It's rare for any individual to know better than a group of individuals.

I also hope you'll see that group decision-making can be learned. As with any set of skills that evolved into a profession over time—like house-building for instance—professional meeting facilitation has come into its own and is a recognized profession today in the United States and the rest of the world. It is growing in popularity and institutionalization. Being a good meeting facilitator is not an ability that you either have or don't have. It's a skill that can be learned. And it's a skill the world needs.

PART I

THE BASICS

CHAPTER 1

What Is a Good Group Decision?

A GROUP DECISION is any decision that affects a group of two or more people regardless of how it was made. Whether decided by one of the members, most of the members, or all of the members, group decisions affect each member of the group.

Group decision-making is everywhere. We all do group decision-making in thousands of different ways in thousands of different types of groups. We are citizens of our country, states, counties, and towns. We participate in these government-defined groups by voting and by making our voices heard in countless ways to our elected representatives.

GROUP DECISION-MAKING IS EVERYWHERE.

We are also members of communities: neighborhood communities, online communities, think-the-same-way communities, dog park communities, lunch-at-the-same-place communities, commuting communities, and groups of friends. Our behavior and our voices influence the decisions of these groups no matter how informal they may seem.

Then there are the corporations, trade associations, unions, political parties, churches, clubs, and charities where we need to make good decisions. As shareholders, employees, and members of these groups, we have votes and other influences. And there are the small groups that many of us are members of: the nonprofit board of directors, the town council or committee, or the team at work. In such small groups we know each other and we work together and we make decisions together in formal ways.

There are many group decisions but few *good* group decisions. First of all, good group decisions achieve what they set out to achieve. They accomplish. They make things better for people. Sometimes "making things better" means that bad things are prevented or that things are not as bad as they would have been without the decision. Second of all, good group decisions result in people getting along better and being happier.

PROFIT AND PEACE

For a group decision to be considered *good*, it needs to result in both profit and peace.

When I use the word *profit*, I'm not talking about just financial profit. I'm talking about a broader definition of the term: a valuable return on investment, getting more back than you put in, and other benefits. In lay terms, when things get better for the group overall, that's what profit is.

Profit can result in a few different forms. The first is that things are better, and that's generally what we think of as profit.

The wealth of the group (such as a company or a family) as a whole increases. Basically, the group has more money as a result of the decision. Money is easy to see and count. But for the non-profit organization or community group that makes decisions that increase their mission impact, that's profit too. My definition of profit in this book is that the good things we get from a decision are worth more than what we put in to make it happen. It's not a *good* group decision if the benefits don't outweigh the costs.

Profit also results when the rate of bad stuff happening slows down. If you are losing money, a decision to lose it at a slower rate is a good decision. Good group decisions change the slopes of downward trends. During the COVID-19 pandemic, for example, thousands of decisions were made by groups to prevent things from being worse than they might otherwise have been. Communities made decisions to close schools and limit social gatherings, decisions that resulted in the slowing of the spread of COVID-19.

1. SLOWING A BAD TREND IS GOOD

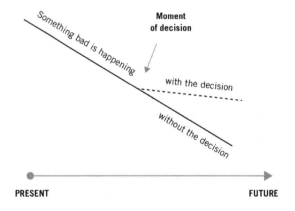

The decision does not make things better, but it's still good because it prevents an even worse outcome.

Another example: Carbon dioxide is accumulating in the atmosphere where it contributes to air pollution in the greenhouse effect or global warming. Any decision made to slow the rate of this trend—even the decision to put solar panels on my own house—can be characterized as a *good* decision because it lessens bad impacts for a group of people (the group of Earth residents).

BUT A GROUP SHOULDN'T SIMPLY AIM TO BECOME MORE PROFITABLE.

Good group decisions are also highly efficient, which contributes to profitability. The process of making good group decisions doesn't waste people's time or the group's money. This doesn't mean that good group-decision processes are always quick or require little investment. Often the investment of time and effort is huge. Good group-decision processes are sized in proper proportion to the stakes, and the process investment is always worth it.

For any group, meeting the profit standard means the following:

- Decisions come with real results that the group can see and feel.

- Because of the decision, more good accrues to the group than bad.

- The return to the group is greater than what they invested in the decision-making process.

But a group shouldn't simply aim to become more profitable. If a truly *good* group decision is made, people in the group will get along with each other better—they will move toward *peace*. A good group decision is an investment in social equity. People feel a greater sense of standing and respect for each other. People feel better than they did before the decision about being a part of the team. Members of the group feel more at peace with themselves and with participating in the group. In addition, the group as a whole becomes stronger and more highly functioning. Each decision, those that are truly good, builds the capacity of the group and leaves the group better off than before the decision.

Not every single member need feel more peaceful—maybe a small minority are disgruntled—yet good group decisions improve the overall peace of the group. People generally get along better and are happier than before the decision. And these things—the peace-generating aspects of good group process—bode well for the next decision and the next one after that. Peace-making **MAKING PEACE IS HARDER THAN MAKING WAR—OR MAKING PROFIT.** is an investment in future decisions. It's organizational development. When good group decisions are made, groups get stronger and more effective.

2. BENEFITS OF GOOD GROUP DECISIONS

BENEFITS OF
GOOD GROUP DECISIONS

PROFIT   PEACE

More wealth,   Bad trends   People get   The group
more impact   slow down   along better gets better

By the way, good group decision processes are
efficient and don't waste people's time.

So why are good group decisions so hard to achieve? One reason is because achieving *the peace standard* is really hard. It requires hard work and discipline and discomfort. It requires short-term sacrifice for long-term benefit. It requires know-how. It requires investment. Being mad at my neighbor is usually easier than talking to my neighbor. Making bad assumptions about someone or a class of people is easier than trying to really understand them. Making peace is harder than making war, or making profit.

Sometimes in a group, your goal is to get along with others and sometimes it's personal achievement. Ideally both happen simultaneously most of the time. Yet when these two are in tension—when you can't decide if your own interests or the group's interests are more important—lean toward the group. It works best to let go of the desire to get your own way and build a desire to get along with others.

A good group decision makes an investment in the members of the group and strengthens our ability to make our next group decision more peacefully. Good group decisions result in feeling better about our neighbors, not worse. Ultimately, good group decisions help us feel better about ourselves. When we participate in a true good group decision, we make peace with ourselves and with our role in the group. We're ready for more.

An Alternative to Hammering It Out

Here in Maine, I worked with an organization of about two hundred employees. Most were unionized and had a long history of traditional collective bargaining. Let's say they are a manufacturing company and do metal fabrication. As each contract's term came to a close, union and management representatives would come to the table to hammer out a new agreement.

I use the term hammer out because the process was destructive, adversarial, and strength-based. Whoever had the bigger hammer got the most in the agreement. In simplest terms, management's hammer was its ability to provide jobs (and wages) and the union's hammer was its ability to withhold labor (strike).

The collective bargaining process typically began with each side coming to the table with its own (artificially inflated) demands. Then a process of trading concessions began until a bare-bones agreement remained, containing the absolute minimum that both sides could live with and that neither side was happy with.

When the company hired a new human resources director who had previously done collective bargaining a different way (interest-based bargaining), she asked me to facilitate this type of bargaining at the company. Each side, management and union, selected a negotiating team of three people to represent their respective collective interests. Nothing new there. But everything was new from that point forward.

Rather than beginning with each side stating their *demands,* we began with each side stating their *concerns.* Rather than each side insisting on what they thought the solutions should be, each side stated and *wrote down* what they saw as problems. All problems then became shared problems, and a new ethic emerged:

"If this is a problem for you, it's a problem for us. Let's solve it together."

Instead of predetermined solutions, accusations, or demands, in each case we made sure that we first understood the problem. This forced both sides to look at each other and understand what things were like for the other side. It provided solid ground for true win-win solutions.

continued

Rather than months of highly contentious meetings, we had a few days of enjoyable meetings. We ate pizza together for dinner three Wednesdays in a row. We worked through a simple process of understanding and defining each problem, brainstorming solutions, and coming to conclusions. Sure, the sides did some horse-trading. They made some concessions. But they maintained respect and a sincere desire for an agreement that would profit, or benefit, both sides. And that's what they got.

And they also got along better—achieved peace—as a result of the process. I'm told that the workplace atmosphere is better now and when conflicts arise, each side now has the group decision-making tools to solve them, tools that they learned and established during the interest-based bargaining process.

WHAT GOOD GROUP DECISIONS LOOK LIKE

Sometimes the benefits of good group decisions take time to manifest. Sometimes decisions are made that cause pain in the short term but bring comfort in the long term. We should not judge the value of decisions too quickly. The worth of a group decision is not based just on what happens in the days or weeks right after the decision, but over the life of the decision's impact. This point is critical because we often expect fast results at the expense of long-term gains. Opponents who don't see immediate benefits are quick to argue, "See, that was a bad decision!" Yet to truly evaluate the worth of a group decision we need to evaluate its net effect for as long as it impacts people.

3. LIFE CYCLE OF A DECISION

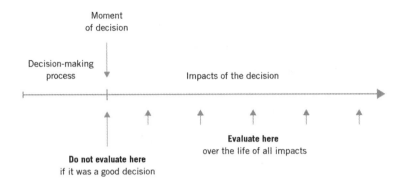

A good group decision should result in net profit for the group of people affected over the entire life of the decision. However, that does not mean that every single member of the group necessarily becomes better off; it means that *most* members of the group—the group as a whole—become better off.

WHEN A GOOD DECISION LOOKS BAD

Since the Grateful Dead's founding in 1965, their fans have been known to freely record their concerts. This practice initially caused tension between those who said, "We need to protect the ownership of our music!" and those who said, "Aw, let the fans record and share it—the music is for everyone!" It wasn't until the 1980s that the band officially decided on its policy of allowing fans to do what they had always done—freely record and share their music.

Immediately following the decision to officially allow concert recordings, commercial record sales declined. The decision looked bad. But over time fans made and shared thousands of recordings and—counterintuitively—the fan base mushroomed. Grateful Dead fans were extremely loyal—in part because the band "gave away their music." These fans bought Grateful Dead concert tickets by the thousands and the band went on to be hugely successful, earning more gross revenue than any other American rock band in the decade of the 1990s.[5] The positive consequences of the free recording decision have spilled way beyond the owners, employees, and vendors. We all get to listen to hundreds of Grateful Dead shows!

WHEN A BAD DECISION LOOKS GOOD

It can happen the other way too. The decision to build the Fukushima Daiichi Nuclear Power Plant on the coast of Japan seemed like a good idea at the time and for the first forty years of its life it provided electricity for its customers and profit for its owners. But its proximity to the ocean during the 2011 earthquake and tsunami led to disaster, and we now have a changed view of the original decision. That fateful decision is still affecting people besides the owners and customers, and it will impact countless people and their families for a very long time to come. Unfortunately, many decisions resulting in environmental degradation look like this—good for the short term but disastrous over time.

---

5   "Was the Grateful Dead the Most Important American Band of All Time?," SavingCountry Music.com, July 5, 2015, https://www.savingcountrymusic.com/was-the-grateful-dead-the -most-important-american-band-of-all-time/.

THE LONG VIEW

When a decision means that one group profits at the expense of another group—including at the expense of future generations—it is not a good group decision. Some decisions simply move goodness (or badness) from one group to another group. If I am in the gaining group it might seem like a good idea in the short term, but in the long term, no matter who the other group is, we all share the outcome. We are all ultimately part of a larger group—the group of human beings. And when some of us are oppressed or disadvantaged, the larger group as a whole will ultimately be hurt as well.

Evaluating the worth of any decision is not a simple matter, and oversimplifying a decision often provides rationale for making a bad one. A nonprofit might say, "If we do this, it'll help our finances, so let's do it." But really what the nonprofit cares about is ending hunger or conserving nature. A decision based on finances alone is oversimplified. It can also happen in the for-profit world: "Hey, if we do this, it will help the bottom line for our first quarter finances." Of course, investors want to see the bottom-line profit improved as quickly as possible. But making an oversimplified short-term decision could hurt the bottom line in the long run. They could underinvest in something that comes back to bite them later or they could cut a corner on something that results in a safety or an environmental crisis. Good group decisions consider the immediate impact on those who will be directly affected, but they also consider the long-term impact on a wider group of people. Good group decisions are for the long haul, so for that reason, we try not to oversimplify or rush them.

DECISION-MAKING IN THE PRIVATE AND PUBLIC SECTORS

A for-profit corporation generally measures profit (success) by looking at the bottom line or the financial profit that it is making over a period of time. It's a simple, universally accepted, and easy-to-evaluate standard. In the nonprofit world, the test of success is "mission impact." Financial profit is not the focus, nor should it be. Nonprofits want the money that comes in to go back out into the field for the good of society.

When it comes to good group decisions, however, both for-profit and nonprofit organizations have to meet the profit and peace standards. If a decision does not help its group become more peaceful and more profitable (again, not necessarily in the financial sense), it is not a *good* group decision.

Here are some examples from companies and nonprofit organizations I've worked with that illustrate what I mean about measuring the profitability (net value) of good group decisions differently. And incidentally, the peace standard is also achieved in each of the next examples. People get along better and communities are improved by virtue of these decisions.

A manufacturing plant I've worked with on the coast of Maine imports seaweed from all over the world and extracts carrageenan, which is added to many commercial food products as an emulsifier or preservative. The extraction process leaves tons of seaweed waste that the company used to truck off to the local landfill, after paying fees to the city. Several years ago, the company decided to seek an alternative use for the leftover seaweed and found an economical way to turn it into fertilizer for farm fields. Because of that good group decision, the company's profits rose. Farmers loved the fertilizer and began purchasing it, and the company is no longer paying city fill fees. This company made decisions that helped its profitability, the community, and the environment all at the same time.

In a similar vein, a manufacturing factory in Maine (also a client) requires a huge volume of No. 6 fuel oil, an industrial-grade diesel imported from far away. The company made a good group decision to add scrap tires into its fuel mix. Car and truck tires burn well and can be sourced locally. And they are cheaper—even with the added cost of having to cut them up on-site. Used tires became a significant portion of the fuel used to fire the kiln and the company's profitability increased as a result. The extra environmental bonus was the reuse of the tires. The extra community bonus was that the "fuel" was purchased locally.

On the nonprofit side, the mission of my local land trust is to "preserve, protect, and steward the cherished landscapes and rich natural resources of our communities, to provide access for recreation, and to support local agriculture and other traditional land uses, now and for generations to come."[6] Several years ago in support of this mission, the land trust made a good group decision and bought a farm—a good-sized farm by Maine standards. It engaged a farming family to move into the old house and work the land and set up a mechanism for the family to have financial stability and plan for retirement. Today, the farm is home to a successful private business, a thriving community garden, a weekly farmers market, several events, and a public labyrinth (a way to walk a really long distance in a really small amount of space and be peaceful and calm and contemplative). And, of course, a large amount of land is protected from development.

---

6   Mission statement of the Brunswick-Topsham Land Trust, https://www.btlt.org/mission.

These good group decisions made by the board of directors significantly increased the land trust's mission impact.

And in the case of two Maine summer camps—one for girls and one for boys—their missions were similar: to educate youth and build character in a challenging but safe outdoor environment. The girl's camp was on one side of the lake, the boy's camp on the other. But the girl's camp had fallen into disuse and disrepair. The board of trustees was trying to figure out how to keep the place alive. The boys camp, on the other hand, was doing so well that it was looking for ways to expand, such as developing new facilities. I served as the neutral facilitator for the two camps as they talked about how they could collaborate. They finished their discussions by agreeing to fully merge the two organizations into one. Because of this good group decision, each organization was substantially able to increase its mission impact. The boys camp increased its mission impact. The girls camp came back to life. The final agreement was signed on a boat in the middle of the lake.

CHAPTER 2

Ways of Making Group Decisions

WHEN YOU THINK of a group of people making decisions together, you probably think of majority rule. And that's usually how it happens in the United States. We have a strong ethic of majority rule decision-making here. From US senators deciding the federal budget to teenagers deciding what pizza to order, the question is almost always "How many people want _____?" It's easy to do and it makes intuitive sense that we as a group should do what most of us want. And, of course, there are many variations in how majority rule is done, including majorities representing majorities (think representative democracy). The notion of majority rule is embedded in American culture.

In many cases, however, group decisions are made by a single person or "one decider"—the boss, the captain, the mom.

Many of us join groups such as a company or a sports team or a military unit where we fully expect a single person to make decisions for us. We agree to follow a leader and do what that leader says. Yet there are two variations of a single person deciding for others; the first is a consensual relationship like those described above and the second is a person imposing decisions on others. For example, it's the teacher deciding things for the children, or the judge deciding the fate of a criminal. Yet it's also the master directing the slave and other instances of forced oppression.

A third broad type of decision-making is when everyone in the group agrees. Sometimes it's called consensus or unanimity, where every member has to agree and where every member has a veto. This is the hardest kind of group decision to achieve and the longest to last. To get full agreement it's important to deliberately encourage and include all perspectives, and try to accommodate all concerns. It's a much higher standard and harder to achieve than majority rule. This type works well for small groups like the owners of a house or a business, or like the five members of the United Nations Security Council.

In the next sections, we'll look at each type more closely, but the following chart outlines each method along a spectrum of how easy to difficult it is to use and the factors that can help determine which method would be best to use.

4. WHEN TO USE WHAT METHOD

	One Decider	Majority Rule	All Agree
Task at hand	Implemenation	Planning and implementation	Planning
Length of impact	Short	Medium	Long
Width of impact	Few	Medium	Many
How much time to decide	Quick	Moderate	Ample

MAJORITY RULE: NEVER PERFECT AND ALWAYS STRESSED

Majority rule decision-making has many benefits. For one thing, majority rule decisions are fairly quick and easy to make. Just take a vote. Done. Another benefit is that there is something inherently logical about letting most of us decide for all of us. It fits with the principle of "the most good for the most people." These two benefits make majority rule extremely practical and popular.

Yet the execution of majority rule has never been easy. No decision-making method ever is; yet majority rule decision-making is particularly fraught with challenges *after* the decision is made.

Perhaps the greatest fault of majority rule decision-making is that there's always a minority out there trying to undermine the decision and trying to win the next decision. It's always a competition, and the competition doesn't end when the vote is taken; it just starts a new competition for the next vote.

Another problem with majority rule is that it has historically applied to a majority of a subset; that is, not all people were allowed to vote. At the founding of the United States, for instance, only white male landowners were allowed to vote. So it was a majority of that group of people (a small minority of all adults living in the country at the time) who were empowered to make decisions on behalf of the new nation.

Confounding the problem of majority rule always being a battle between the minority and the majority is that wealthier people have disproportionate influence over voters. This is because voters are influenced by advertising and media, and wealthy people are better positioned to buy advertising and influence the media. Not only that, but in the United States wealthy people and corporations are allowed to influence politics through political action committees, which mask where donations are coming from. The right of corporations to donate huge amounts of money and remain anonymous is also supported by the Citizens United Supreme Court decision.[7] Consequently, decisions are often made not by a majority of voters but by a majority of money. This dynamic is especially exaggerated in the United States, where we have the highest wealth divide right now, or biggest difference between the rich and the poor, that we've had in the last hundred years.

Another set of challenges for majority rule have been brought by the internet. I used to think the internet would be really great for democracy. A good democracy requires a well-informed electorate, right? Yay! We are going be well informed like never before!

But unlike when we used to read our local print newspaper

---

7   Citizens United v. Federal Election Commission, 558 U.S. 310 (2010).

or watch the network news on TV, we now get to choose who informs us. We read online newspapers and blogs we already agree with. We unfollow social media friends we don't agree with. Rather than become better informed about all perspectives, we have become stronger believers in our own perspectives, reinforced by an endless stream of supporting media that we arrange to have sent to ourselves.

While more and more information is available, we create fewer and fewer opportunities to get together with different-minded people to talk about it. This results in huge opportunities to misunderstand each other, and when we don't understand the perspective of "the other side," we seem to be happy to manufacture reasons for why they think the way they do.

As a result of these dynamics and other forces, majority rule is not working very well in the United States right now. And we know it. Many of us have checked out. Some people have lost faith in the current system of government and so they are not participating in a system that seems increasingly out of touch and ineffective. Majority rule decision-making is not as awesome as many of us once thought it was.

Apart from public voting and government decision-making, majority rule is also used by many for-profit and nonprofit corporate boards throughout the country. And in those settings too, many of the same challenges mentioned previously apply. Shareholder or member voting rates are ridiculously low, and in private settings too, wealth can have a huge influence over voting and outcomes. In most majority rule settings—especially in the United States due to our capitalist disposition—the power is not with a majority of the people but with a majority of the wealth. This is a problem.

THE ONE DECIDER AND THE BIG IF

One-decider decisions happen when the official rule for the group is that a single person decides for everyone. The benefits of this method can be enormous if the single decider truly acts in the interests of the group, rather than being driven by self-interest. Benevolent dictatorship is perhaps the best method of group decision-making. A benevolent dictator is open-minded to all available information and all good ideas, even if not their own. A benevolent dictator carefully considers all options and chooses the one that will most likely bring the most benefits to the most people over the life of the decision. A benevolent dictator acts far more efficiently than any other decision-making group could act.

But there is a big *if.* The benefits of this method can be enormous *if* the single decider truly acts in the interests of the group. But that very rarely happens. Sometimes we think it's going to happen, but then things change. Actually, we almost always think it's going to happen. Politicians and leaders tell us in great detail and with great conviction how they are going to act in the best interests of the group. And then things change.

We have millions of examples from history of single deciders making decisions that doomed groups. Single deciders often develop a delusional mindset that tells them they deserve more power. Many single deciders think God ordained them. Single deciders often grab power rather than earn it. They feel entitled to take what's not theirs. An extreme example of this is when a tyrant conquers a new land and forces people into servitude, or encourages genocide. Yet we can also find tyrant single deciders right among us in all walks of life and in many degrees. Whether good leaders or bad leaders, the deciders that I'm thinking of include the bosses, the heads of a household, or the military commanders. These are the deciders among us.

I knew a manager who regularly called her team together and said something like, "OK, I'm going to decide about this matter next week. I've looked at all the options, and I'm leaning toward Option A. And here's why." And she would explain why. "But before I decide I want to hear your opinions. You are my best thinkers on this topic and this decision affects all of you and the people who work for you. And after I decide I want your support. OK. What do you think?"

Team members would give their opinions. Some would ask questions. Some would give opposing opinions. Some would give supporting opinions. The manager would ask questions to further her understanding. She let them bounce their ideas off each other and come up with new ideas on the spot. The manager ended the meeting, and then a week later she decided and told everyone her decision.

While made by a single person, this was a *group* decision because it affected a group of people, the team members, and all their subordinates. We wouldn't know for sure until it was fully implemented, but this seemed likely to be a *good* group decision because of the following points: The manager gathered the right group of people to give her the best possible advice. She framed the decision by stating who would make the decision and when. She created a space for shared learning for her to learn from her team members and for them to learn from each other. She encouraged creative thinking and encouraged new ideas. And then she made the decision and conveyed the decision just as she said she would.

CONSENSUS: MOST DURABLE
AND HARDEST TO MANUFACTURE

Consensus decision-making is when a large percentage of those affected by the decision are invited to engage in crafting the decision, not just to vote on it. This method is the most rarely used of all the methods available, and it is far and away the most difficult. It is often hard for an outsider or newcomer to figure it out. A person can easily get bogged down in the process to the point where it's intolerable if they don't have the time or the patience.

CONSENSUS DOESN'T MEAN CASUAL. Many consensus decision-making processes don't seem to end in a decision at all but rather seem to end in conflict or frustration. Consensus decision-making has a bad reputation in the marketplace. In my cohousing neighborhood we fumbled with consensus decision-making when we were first getting started and learning how to use it, and our fumbles created a lot of conflict. It turned neighbor against neighbor and caused some people to leave the neighborhood. It also scared people from joining us.

Yet the benefits of consensus decision-making are clear, with the chief one being implementation. Once a decision is made, implementation is a breeze. Because every group member supports the decision, there is no minority trying to undermine or reverse the decision. Another benefit is shared understanding. The process of making a decision by consensus is also a process of education. All participants learn about the situation and learn each other's perspectives. Collective understanding is significantly raised and thus makes each step in the process easier and likely better.

A third key benefit is group unity. When we go through a consensus process correctly, by the end of the process we like and respect each other. We have increased enthusiasm for our common goals. We feel even more a part of our group.

But the two biggest challenges with consensus decision-making are that it is often not done very well and it is often applied inappropriately. Consensus doesn't mean casual. Just like any other decision-making process, there is a right and a wrong way to do it. It needs to be well organized. And participants need to know their parts and do them. In fact, since consensus decision-making strives to consider all perspectives and involve so many people, it is even more important that the process be very deliberate and honored. In addition, groups who operate "by consensus" often want to apply consensus to *every* decision. Not every decision is worthy of such an involved process. Certain decisions are best decided by a small group or a single person empowered by the group.

Consensus decisions are most appropriate for those that affect a large number of people over a long time—for instance, a group's mission, values, and strategic plan. Ensuring these types of decisions are widely understood and supported is helpful in the long run so a consensus process is a worthy investment. When consensus is applied to short-lived, limited-scope decisions, it leads to inefficiency and frustration.

THE PROCESS MUST BE WORTH IT

As with any other process, the costs and benefits of a group decision matter. Group decision-making is often criticized as inefficient and a waste of time. Group decisions are most apt to be criticized in an organization where people don't have faith in the management. People called to a meeting or called to participate in a group decision are often disgruntled, skeptical, and critical. They think, "This is going to be a waste of time because they're not going to listen to what I say anyway. They're going to make a decision but they're not going to act on it, and nothing's going to change even though I'm going to spend a whole afternoon on this thing." I was working with a nature center that wanted to ask its staff for input on the design of a proposed new building. The groundskeeper was invited to this staff meeting. I could tell by his body language that he didn't want to be there. Thought it was a waste of time. Sure enough, about halfway through the meeting he got up and left with an announcement, "I got wood to split."

If the costs of the process are more than the value of the benefits, then it *is* inefficient and it *is* a waste of time. The time that individuals spend working together to make an idea into a reality is extremely valuable. You might calculate the value of that time as the value of my time multiplied roughly by the number of people in the room multiplied by the length of the meeting. And you bet my time is valuable. In fact, I'm not sure there is anything in the world more valuable to me. Probably the most important decision I make every day, every minute, is how to spend my time.

When I'm part of a group of volunteers gathered on a Saturday morning in the school gym to plan Project Graduation, I want efficiency. I want the others to assume that I've got things to do, that people are waiting for me, and I assume the same about others' time. I don't mind being there; indeed, I volunteered to help. But if I think my time is being wasted, I'm apt to become disinterested and disgruntled. I'm not likely to contribute positively, and I might even contribute negatively by telling others that the project is a waste of time.

And it's not just the cost of people's time that counts in determining if a decision is truly a good one. We also need to calculate the emotional tolls, unintended consequences, damaged relationships, and any other forms of discontent.

I'm not saying that these things should (or can) be avoided at all costs, but group processes that generate negative consequences need to achieve higher standards of group benefits if they are to qualify as truly good group decisions. The *profit standard* is hard to achieve.

GOOD GROUP DECISIONS ARE ALWAYS AN INVESTMENT IN A BETTER FUTURE.

It's fine to have a really big and long and hard process that solves a really big problem for lots of people. But you don't want to have a really big and long and hard process that solves a small problem for a few people. Good group decisions have to be made skillfully, with the right-sized process, and maximize the value of the participants' contributions.

Good group decisions are always an investment in a better future. Improving the efficiency of group decision-making processes—lowering the costs relative to the benefits—is critical to increasing the number of groups out there making *good* group decisions.

CHAPTER 3

Culture Wins Every Time

THE MAINE INFECTION Prevention Collaborative was a group of twenty-eight infection prevention officers (one from each hospital in Maine) who came together once a month to share techniques and compare notes. During a meeting I facilitated for them, the caterers came into the back of the room and set up a beautiful buffet as we neared lunchtime. We had been meeting for hours, and I knew people were anxious for the meeting to end. They were hungry. The moment I said, "Meeting adjourned," all twenty-eight got up and formed an orderly line—not at the beautiful buffet table, but at the little hand sanitizer dispenser on the wall. Every one of them waited in that line first, sanitized their hands, and then went for the food. And this was long before COVID-19, by the way.

Their actions were an important part of their group culture. They believed in preventing the spread of germs. It's what they did, and doing so in front of each other reinforced their culture. When I went to get my lunch, you bet that I went for the hand sanitizer first. I wanted to fit in. I wanted to show them that I honored their culture.

When I facilitated a meeting for leaders of the Maine Emergency Management Agency, the host made an announcement before I was introduced. "In the event of an emergency," she said loudly and clearly, "we will evacuate via the doors to my left and right," signaling like an airline attendant, "and we will assemble in the front parking lot at Pole F. There are sixteen people in this room. I will take attendance at Pole F in the event of an evacuation." And then in a lighter tone she proceeded, "And now I would like to introduce our facilitator . . ." It's what they did—it's who they were—based on what they believed. By beginning their meeting with this ritual, they reinforced their culture.

WE ARE HOW WE ACT

Aristotle is often attributed with saying "We are what we repeatedly do." Indeed, you might say. The word indeed means "in reality," something that's actually acted out, not just thought about. In my view, a group's culture is a combination of what the members think and what they do. A group's culture is its customs and beliefs, its characteristics and knowledge, its way of life. It's the attitudes the group has and the steps it takes together. The following are some examples of actions and rituals from various group meetings I have facilitated:

- The Maine Council of Churches begins meetings with a prayer.

- The FMC manufacturing plant begins with a safety reminder.

- The Two Echo 4H Club begins with the 4H pledge.

- The Maine Coast Waldorf School faculty begin with a song or a verse.

- Meetings of bankers have pastries on white dishes with white tablecloths, and people wear suits and ties.

- The Maine Organic Farmers and Gardeners Association meetings begin with members sharing pole beans and carrots picked that morning—everyone takes a few as the basket comes around—and people wear flannel shirts.

- At a board of trustees meeting for Camp Agawam, a traditional Maine summer camp for boys, we met at the camp on a hot August day and I was warned in advance to wear shorts. After the meeting we jumped in the lake. It's what they did.

Culture is coveted. We want it. We like the idea of being part of a culture. We honor and perpetuate our cultural traditions with special holidays, special meals, special foods at special meals, and special ways those meals are prepared and eaten. Traditions like decorations, seating arrangements, and spoken words are practiced the same way, time after time and place after place, among all people with a shared culture. Groups of people—whether nations or companies or families—go to great lengths to demonstrate the culture they have.

Cultures slide over and under each other, interacting and influencing each other. And no single person is part of a single culture. Sometimes I'm part of the suit-and-tie set. And sometimes I'm part of the flannel shirt set.

Some cultures are part of my core identity and I don't ever veer far from them. For instance, I am a Mainer. Even when I am in a very different culture such as Europe or New York City, it's hard to pretend that I'm not from Maine. Most of the time, for instance, I look just like that guy in the L.L.Bean catalog.

ATTITUDES ARE INDIVIDUAL. CULTURE BELONGS TO THE GROUP.

An attitude is carried by an individual group member. A culture is carried by the group as a whole. A group's culture is the aggregate of individual attitudes. Group culture is shaped over time by individual attitudes, just as individual attitudes are shaped by the group's culture. And it's the group culture that an outsider goes by when assessing a group (what they do)—not their written intentions or mission statement written on paper (what they say).

"Dana, look at this!" I said to my daughter, pointing to some words in the brochure of the out-of-state college we were visiting. She thought she might like to apply here. We were sitting on a bench in the quad taking a break from all the walking. A beautiful summer day. I was looking down at the brochure and the words were really impressive. It seemed like a perfect fit for my daughter and her aspirations. She was looking up at the students walking by. "Dana, look at this!" I repeated as I nudged her and tried to call her attention to the brochure. "But Dad," she said, pausing to look at me, knowing I wasn't going to like what she had to say, "I don't like what they're wearing." Done. Moving on. Back in the car and on to the next college. There was no way that my logical assessment based on brochure words was going to compete with my daughter's cultural assessment based on fashion. Culture wins every time.

Culture is slippery, unpredictable, and very hard to define. People can try to capture and describe the culture of people or places with words, or photos, or video and audio, but to really understand a group's culture you have to experience it. In fact, some would argue that the very definition of culture is that which you *cannot* capture with words and photos and video and audio. Culture is the stuff between those things that you can capture. It's a feeling. This is precisely why in order to find the perfect-fit college, it helps if you drive for miles and actually get out of the car and get a feel for the place.

A group's culture is what ultimately attracts people to a group or repels people away from a group. Culture guides the attitudes and behaviors of individuals way more than written rules and laws. Effective leaders know that the key to real and lasting change is group culture. If you want your group to change, you've got to change the culture. Leaders also know that you have to call out the culture that you do want and don't want. They point out and criticize and even shame bad examples, and they praise and—this is the best of all—model good examples. They actively demonstrate how they want others to behave. They promote people who are doing things in line with desired culture.

New leaders can bring new goals, new objectives, and new strategies but without actual cultural change, those goals, objectives, and strategies don't have a chance. Perhaps you have heard the popular expression attributed to Peter Drucker: "Culture eats strategy for breakfast."

Your Days Are Numbered

I was hired by a manufacturing company to lead a series of workshops designed to help change the corporate culture. Imagine the start of the first session in a nondescript corporate training room. I was at the front—the guy with the tie because I had been hired by management—when the workers started filing in. I could tell that they didn't want to be in the training. They sat down without talking to each other. I could see the culture was "keep your head down, don't say anything, don't call attention to yourself, just get through this." I started by taking off my tie. After a while I got them talking. Then a story came up: First day on the job for the new warehouse supervisor, he comes across a couple guys without their safety glasses on. Like all employees, he had a responsibility to correct any safety violation on the spot so he says, "Hey, I know I'm new here, but I'm pretty sure we're all supposed to be wearing safety glasses in the warehouse." The two guys didn't take kindly to this and one of them said, "OK, your days are numbered." And the two guys turned and left the warehouse.

So much to say about this little story:

1. The new warehouse supervisor had learned that there is a culture of reciprocity/revenge.

2. He had learned that there were two cultures in his new workplace: what the book says and what really happens in the warehouse.

3. Was he going to side with the written rules of management or try to fit into the culture of the warehouse workers? This is often a huge question for a middle manager. In this case, I'm not sure what he decided.

Ideally, dilemmas like this (and the associated drama!) would not distract employees if the warehouse culture was truly aligned with the on-the-books culture. A new employee wouldn't have to make such choices. The best organizations operate with just one culture. Everyone knows what it is. You can see it on the floor and you can read it in the book. Same thing.

ARE YOU A CULTURE KEEPER OR A CULTURE CHANGER?

Groups must change if they want to survive and thrive. We know this by looking at ecology and anthropology. Yet groups must retain beliefs and customs in order to hold themselves together and grow strong in spirit and number. Talented leaders identify what to keep and what to change. They also define what aspects of the culture are important to reinforce and what aspects need nudging in new directions. Groups want things to stay the same, yet they also need things to change. Culture keepers and culture changers are in tension, and we need both. Gifted leaders—those able to discern what to keep and what to change—need not be in actual leadership positions. Culture keepers and culture changers are among us at all levels and in all places.

Culture keepers study and model traditions. They cook family recipes and visit ancestral places and wear the old fashions and talk the old ways. They fight to keep traditions alive. They pass along stories that they learned from their elders. Walk into any meeting for the first time and you immediately begin to see its traditions—kept visible by the culture keepers.

Culture changers are the apparent rebels, the ones pushing for things to be done in new ways. They practice new ways of thinking on the fringes and out of sight to both perfect their theories and build momentum. They bring new technologies and new manufacturing methods and new music and new dance moves. They compel changed attitudes and behaviors by showing us what fun it is to do things differently and how change can make our lives better. They tell stories about the future and work one convert at a time to change the larger culture.

Culture keepers tell stories too, about the past, and how those lessons learned are relevant today. Stories are kernels of truth passed on in colorful ways that help us understand the truths they contain, and most of us relate to stories much better than we relate to facts and figures. Have you ever heard this phrase? "All stories are true, and some of them really happened." It's actually not so important that a story really happened. What's more important is how a story is like *my* story, like *our* story— and how the truth it contains about the human experience is your truth and my truth in the same story. Stories indoctrinate people into the culture of an organization, for either good or bad. Here's an example.

I knew a leader who called a weekly in-person meeting for 9:00 a.m. and showed up at 8:50 every time. For ten minutes before every meeting, she chitchatted with people and she was hugely influential in what stories she told and what questions she asked. She set the culture just by how she participated in conversation with her employees. She heard their stories, and with her body language and reactions, she encouraged stories that aligned with her vision of the corporate culture.

In addition to building culture on the inside, we build culture when we read and listen to stories of other groups like our own. We praise and promote stories that ring true, wherever they come from. It's by telling and hearing stories that we come to under-standing. It's through stories that we create culture and community.

SHARED CULTURE MAKES US A GROUP

Groups gather around what they have in common or what they hope to have in common. If I and another person have absolutely nothing in common—no characteristics currently in common and no future desires in common—we are not a group.

The wonderful thing about looking forward and wanting the same thing is that even though we might not have anything in common right now, we can make it so we have something in common: a common vision. Even though we might not *have* the same things, we can *want* the same things. Even though we might make war over what we have or don't have in common, we can make peace over what we want in common. **EVEN THOUGH WE MIGHT NOT HAVE THE SAME THINGS, WE CAN WANT THE SAME THINGS.** Even though we might compete over what we currently have or don't have, we can collaborate for what we want in common. In spite of the current tensions *against* each other, we can make future profits and peace *with* each other. We can look forward to the same point on the horizon.

Working for a good company or a good cause gives us a sense of identity, a sense of place, a sense of belonging. In the compa-nies we work for, we may come from different places and create products that go to different places, but our company is the one place we have in common. Humans want to belong. We natu-rally look for things in common with others—things we have in common or things we want in common. We desire to be part of something bigger, deeper, and greater than ourselves. We want to keep good company.

For instance, whenever arriving in a new place, we look for signs that we belong. When we are strangers at a gathering, we immediately try to figure out what we have in common with the others. We look for people we know. We look for signs that we fit in. The more we find we have in common, the more comfortable we feel.

Strangers meeting for the first time often talk about the weather or their travels to the meeting place. Sometimes they ask each other, "Did you find the place OK?" Or "Did you have any trouble getting here?" They begin conversations about things they are likely to have in common. We all had to travel here. That topic is a pretty safe bet for finding something in common. Other examples: "Beautiful day today, huh?" Or "This is a nice room, isn't it?" They talk about these things because commonality is highly likely and they can immediately develop a sense of belonging. Facilitated meetings often have an icebreaker activity that helps participants find commonalities and encourages a sense of belonging, which ultimately encourages commitment.

The community builders among us (anyone working to make the group stronger, including culture changers and keepers) *proactively build* commonalities and create a sense of belonging. They cook the meals and invite the guests and organize the concerts and other events that gather people together. Community builders tell stories that allow us to see our common past and common experiences, stories that hold our common visions for the future, and that help form the strong foundation needed for collaborative decisions.

PART II

ATTITUDES

CHAPTER 4

The Critical Five

GOOD GROUP DECISION-MAKING has just as much to do with what people believe as what steps they follow. I have seen many groups set up rules and take steps perfectly, but their actions didn't result in peace and profit because one or more of the decision makers didn't have a helpful attitude.

For a group to make good decisions, the disposition of each participant matters. That is, the beliefs that each participant brings with them to the table have a profound impact on the group's chance of success. Good group decisions require much more than good rules and mechanics. What each participant believes, in their hearts, is a big deal for good group decisions.

Certain attitudes can work against good group decisions and are downright counterproductive for group profit and peace. For instance, a good group decision is unlikely if even one decision maker believes that they are better than the others, or that they know best, or that the group's mission is hopeless and destined to fail. Good group decisions are almost impossible when one or more of the decision makers are too closed-minded, self-centered, pessimistic, stubborn, or arrogant.

And certain attitudes work in favor of group decisions as well. I have come to believe that five attitudes, in particular, are critical to success.

ATTITUDE #1: COMMUNITY FIRST

The notion of group first—putting group interests before individual interests—is a timeless and well-proven attitude. It applies to teams, to companies, to countries, and to species.

If I'm on a basketball team and I set out to score more points than anybody else—to make myself look good—the team may suffer. For one thing, I am preventing the potentially great contributions of others. For another, I might not be that good or I might be having an off night. Others on the team might be way more capable, but if I never let others have the ball, my teammates are going to end up frustrated or angry, regardless of the result.

When you put your own interests over group interests, you might have personal gains in the short run, but the group is destined to lose over the long run. This attitude often comes into play when a person does something that they know will have a negative impact on others in the group. For instance, if I own a piece of property and I pollute the water for my own personal gain, such a violation can help me make more money in the short term because I don't have to invest in a pollution control system. But the people downstream and the wider community will suffer over the long term as a result of my actions. There are many examples of individuals and corporations who try to get away with increasing their gain at community expense: cigarette manufacturers and oxycodone producers who intentionally withhold information, car manufacturers who cheat emissions tests, and anyone who cheats on their taxes.

People who believe in themselves more than they believe in their groups have a hard time with group decision-making. They are typically impatient with group processes, preferring to make decisions independently and impose their will on others. But people who believe in the wisdom of the group—even at the expense of setting personal concerns aside—are much better suited to group decision-making and are almost always more helpful contributors.

The group will profit if the individual members put the group first, but it will crash and burn—and eventually go extinct—if the individual members are concerned more with getting for themselves rather than giving to the group. If you want to help your group make good decisions that result in both peace and profit, put group interests over selfish ones. Believe in *we* over *me*.

For some people, the idea of putting others first is a spiritual conviction. It may be a belief in a god of some sort or a belief in a set of national values or a belief in nature. It is a desire "to do God's will" or to "serve one's country" for the benefit of others or for the environment. People with such beliefs are generally good contributors to their groups.

Yet putting the group first is not just a nice spiritual or religious idea, it's extremely practical if you want your group to last. Putting the group first is an attitude successfully employed by many species the world over. It is particularly easy to see in colonies of insects. The term *superorganism* applies to an organized society made up of several living organisms such as ant and termite colonies and beehives. In many such cases, the individuals cannot survive without the colony. Individuals have specific jobs that support the good of the colony. The colony is able to achieve things that no individual could do on their own. And the colony actually makes group decisions. A colony of bees, for instance, decides as a group on a new location for the hive.[8] Further, individuals in many such colonies will die for the good of the colony—such as the bee that dies after it stings its victim or the termite that explodes itself to poison predators.

There are also scientifically documented examples among bacteria, fungi, plants, and mammals where it's clear that individuals are more concerned with the good of the group than the good of the self. One simple mammalian example is the hyrax, a small groundhog-like animal found throughout Africa and on part of the Arabian Peninsula. When a hyrax spots a leopard looking for food, it alerts the other group members so they can hide while that one hyrax stays out longer to monitor the leopard. Only at the last second does the lookout-hyrax hide after it has put itself at risk to keep the others safe.

When individual members of packs or schools or herds do what is best for the group, the dividends often come back to the individual in terms of shared safety and shared food. Benefits also accrue to the sustainability of one's children and grandchildren and many subsequent generations.

---

8   For more on this, see Honeybee Democracy by Thomas D. Seeley.

INDIVIDUAL ACHIEVEMENT IS NOT THE GOAL

Many of us don't come from this perspective, especially in America. Most of us here in the United States have been raised with a drive toward individual achievement, a general belief that success in life is measured by individual success. And there's a corollary that says: "By the way, your individual success will benefit the group." For instance, if I do well in school and get a good job, I will earn good money and spend that money into the economy, which will help the group (society) as a whole.

A degree of self-interest is fine, even healthy. And so too is a degree of competition that spurs individual achievement and innovation—and ever greater achievements. Self-interest to serve group interests is OK, such as taking care of myself and bettering myself in order to better contribute to my community. Self-interest running roughshod over community interests—an attitude of me first no matter what—is not OK.

I have learned time and time again that when I am in despair, or feeling sorry for myself, or angry at the world, or disappointed in those around me, being mean or taking things from others never fixes the problem. What works for me without fail when I am in despair is to help another person in despair. I get short-lived, hollow satisfaction from taking. I get long-term, genuine satisfaction from giving. This attitude is taking me a lifetime to own, and it's a work in progress for sure. Yet when I have this attitude, it helps me contribute to good group decisions—and to be a happier person. It's circular: keeping myself happy helps my group and helping my group makes me happy.

IS IT *ME* OR IS IT *WE?*

How you answer this question indicates how helpful you might be to making good group decisions. I'm not saying you need be all one way (me) or all the other way (we) all the time. I'm simply saying that when you are in a meeting working with others on a group decision, you're going to do the most good for your group if you put the group first.

To put the group first is to be humble. It's saying, "I am not the most important thing in the universe." It's saying, "I don't always know what's best. Someone else may know better." It is moving forward and going along with the group, even when you don't completely understand or completely agree with where the group is headed. It is putting more faith in the group's wisdom than in your own intellect.

When individual members of a community believe in and contribute to the community, the community flourishes. And when communities flourish, their members are more likely to be happy and satisfied. When people put community interests over self-interests—when they put *we* over *me*—the group becomes more peaceful and more profitable and so do most of the individual members.

As human beings, we have a natural desire to belong; we want to belong to a group. Belonging to groups and being social contributes to our happiness.[9] Of course, many people want to go it alone—in the United States especially we have an over-glorified notion of "independence"—but in my experience such a desire is often the result of irrational fear, social dysfunction, or low self-esteem. Emotionally healthy humans aren't afraid

---

9   "The Science Behind the Smile," *Harvard Business Review*, 2012.

to depend on others or help others, and in return get practical benefits from being connected to other people.

I love it when communities nurture a culture that supports giving to the community. Sometimes it's called civic engagement, or even civic duty. Those who give to the common good are exalted. Those who take from the common good are shamed. In the United States we are good at exalting the soldier who gives their life for their group; yet we are not so good at shaming the person or corporation who takes from the group, such as polluting common natural resources, avoiding taxes, or exploiting workers.

INSIGHT: Credit the Group

Members of the most high-functioning groups are always focused on the success of the group rather than on individual credit or blame. President Harry S. Truman once said, "It is amazing what you can accomplish if you do not care who gets the credit."[10]

Members of these groups don't waste energy accounting for individual credit—or blame. It doesn't matter. High-functioning groups know how to invest contributions—no matter where they come from—into good group decisions. When I believe in my group, I know that in the long run, what is good for the group will be good for me—and will probably exceed anything I could ever have achieved on my own. Here are some characteristics of high-functioning groups:

continued

---

10 https://www.trumanlibraryinstitute.org/truman/truman-quotes/page/5/.

- Members give their ideas and efforts to the group without conditions or lingering ownership.

- Members welcome contributions from others without jealousy or resentment.

- Each member wants to make other members look good. Members show public appreciation for others in the group.

- Members own their share of things gone wrong and credit the group for things gone right.

ATTITUDE #2: ACCEPTANCE

Often the most helpful and healthy attitude for any group's efforts and for individual peace and happiness is acceptance. I accept that it's OK that I may not be getting my way; I accept that the group is organized a certain way or that it's moving in a certain direction—and that's OK; I accept that I don't need to fight to the end for every one of my personal desires at every opportunity. When my attitude is to never give in to a particular way of thinking or a new way doing, I am surely creating turmoil for myself or my group.

It's all fine and good to work hard for a particular outcome, yet when it becomes clear that the group is headed in a different direction, that's the time to lay down my fight and accept the direction of the group. Often, one strategy follows the other. I fight like hell to try to change something and then at some point I try to accept the result. I do the best I can—I put it all out there and leave it all on the field of battle—and then once the battle is over, I let go of the fight and accept the results. That's how I find peace.

Sometimes after the battle is over, I can't let go of the outcome. I want to keep fighting. I seek new fights to overturn the last outcome. And that's OK if my convictions require me to press on and if I'm good with continuing conflict. What's not OK is to complain about the past without trying to change or accept things going forward. Yelling about injustices of "what happened" with no plan to help make things better is a set-up for continued turmoil within yourself and within your group. Instead, I try to tell myself, "That actually happened and this is how things are now." And I try to turn my attention to what I should do now in light of this new reality—who I should be.

Each person has to decide for themselves where the line is in every case. When to fight. When to accept. The point is that every person actually has a choice. Peace is available to each one of us when we are able to make such choices to see things differently.[11]

ATTITUDE #3: GIVE

Communities do not happen by themselves. We have to build them. Any group of decision makers is surrounded by some sort of community. Good communities act as support networks and help each community member be a better person. We build community by giving gifts and looking for giving opportunities.

And we all have gifts to give, of all types. For some, it is one-to-one

---

11 For more on this, see "Two Paths to Peace" in Chapter 16, Ways to Get Along.

giving between group members, like sending a birthday card or offering a ride. Other people give money, time, or something else that is precious or needed at a crucial time. Others make the community space a little more beautiful by adding flowers or helping to make a safer environment. Some play music. Some

COMMUNITY GIVING IS LIKE POTLUCK, NOT POKER. do decorations. Chris, in my cohousing community, is always doing dishes at community events. In every moment he's wondering how to be helpful.

Community giving is "someone shoveled my walk and I don't know who" or "someone left a gift" or "someone did the dishes." Sometimes it's cracking the joke that lightens the mood. Sometimes it is delivering news that needs to be heard. Sometimes it is spontaneous, like a sign I once saw in Blue Hill, Maine, outside a church hall: "Impromptu Christmas Concert. Tonight. 7:30. Please come." Or sometimes it's "let's get a bite to eat after the meeting." Community giving is like potluck, not poker.[12] It's sharing, not competing. It's giving, not getting.

Sometimes it's found in the way in which we interact. Consider the difference between a person standing up at a town meeting and beginning with, "I am a taxpayer of this town and I demand . . . " and another person beginning with, "I am a citizen of this town, and I think . . . " The taxpayer is concerned with what they are getting *from* the town in return for the money they pay in taxes. The citizen has a broader view, recognizing that being a citizen means more than a quid pro quo payment for services. The town government is not a business providing a service

---

12 Colleen Dawicki, Boston Fed Presentation to Working Communities Challenge Grantees, September 4, 2021.

in exchange for taxes. It is an administrator of community goodness. It's where resources get pooled for community good. People
with transactional mindsets like the taxpayer are not as likely to
contribute to good group decisions as the citizens who pay their
taxes with pride.

The problem with transactional (or tit-for-tat) behavior is
that no new benefits are created. Existing benefits are simply
transferred from one person or group to another person or
group. Tit for tat is a common way that people and groups use
to protect their assets or their net worth; that is, they try to
experience no loss in *net* benefits. People of this mindset tend
to be concerned with their rights, ever on guard that they don't
get less than what they think they are due. When people participate in a community from which each member takes more
than they give or expects something in return, the worth of the
community diminishes. Resentment and apathy grow and the
community declines.

On the other hand, when people give just to give, without expecting anything in return, a multiplier effect kicks in.
And that's when the magic happens. Think of churches. People
don't go to church today like they used to. But here in New
England it's always been "the church ladies" who get stuff done
and provide an enormous sense of community. The church
ladies provide support for all manner of community-based
events, and such events bring people together to chitchat and
weave the fabric of shared experience that make communities
resilient.

The church ladies enjoy giving, at least I hope they do. I imagine that each church lady goes to sleep at night feeling a sense
of achievement, contribution, and pride. "I helped bake for that

family's funeral." Or "So good that we got John to the doctor today." Or "Feels good to get the town hall decorated." Simple things but good feelings. I love that feeling of giving to my community. And it's contagious—it becomes the thing to do.

GIVING AS A WAY OF
LIFE BREEDS ABUNDANCE

It seems so simple, even trivial, but it's not: When we focus on giving rather than getting, our group benefits enormously. And you know what? You will get a lot too. You'll receive gifts that you didn't even ask for, didn't even try to get—gifts beyond your imagination.

Unconditional giving is a moral imperative for many people. Many faith communities and other types of communities encourage a morality of unconditional giving because it's the right thing to do. But I'm arguing that it is a practical thing to do if you want your group to make good decisions.

It's like banking. You have to make deposits before making withdrawals. And when lots of people in the community make deposits, the money grows. And if it's a community-minded bank like Bailey Building and Loan in the film *It's a Wonderful Life,* when the money grows, the whole community benefits.

When you are only concerned with what you can get from your community rather than what you can give, you are apt to make withdrawals before making deposits. That puts you in debt. But if you are first concerned with giving and make deposits before withdrawals, that builds your credit and keeps you out in front. You gain credibility with your neighbors. When you ask for a favor, people want to help.

Put giving over getting. Put your community first. And if

others in your community do the same you will likely make good group decisions and have a community that provides benefits beyond your imagination.

AA—Where Community Giving Saves Lives

A fine example of giving without expectation of return is Alcoholics Anonymous (AA), where the twelfth step is about helping others. This ethos of giving is part of the culture of Alcoholics Anonymous and it provides benefits in two ways: giving to others helps the community and it helps the individual.

AA meetings are run by volunteers who show up early and make the coffee and set up the Zoom. Call it volunteer-powered infrastructure. People give willingly—even eagerly—to the group and to each other, and everyone benefits. New wealth is created—social wealth known as goodwill. And it is easy to see in AA and hundreds of other twelve-step programs.

Volunteer service in AA achieves more than getting coffee made. For many it provides a reason to belong; for some it's a reason to live. Giving to the group provides enormous individual benefit. Want to help a struggling person? Give them a meaningful job to do. When I'm struggling, my sense of responsibility to my group might keep me going. When I look for a way to contribute something to my group, I feel better.

By the way, in addition to the AA's twelve steps, did you know there are twelve traditions? The traditions are about how AA runs itself as an organization. It's a pretty great list of principles, beginning with, "Our common welfare should come first."[13]

---

13 https://www.aa.org/assets/en_US/smf-122_en.pdf.

ATTITUDE #4: OWNERSHIP

Am I *a part* of my community or am I *apart* from my community? Do I refer to the group—the government, the company, the neighborhood—as *we* or as *they*? This is not a trivial matter. You might take a moment to consider how you think of your federal, state, and local governments. When you talk about the government with others, or when you talk about your company or your family, do you use the terms *we/us* or *they/them*?

If my attitude is that I am apart from the group and it is a *they*, then I am likely to be discontented and I might even want the group to fail so that my self-righteousness and selfishness are validated. But if I carry an attitude of truly being *part of* my group, then I have a stake in its success. What's good for the group is good for me. I am happy to contribute. I refer to my group as if I were an owner. It's *our* government; not *the* government as if it were something "over there," detached.

When you're faced with a problem to be solved or a task to be done, especially if you are part of a high-functioning group, you might think that *someone else will take care of it*. Yet it's important that *you* take the initiative for achieving group tasks. You shouldn't need to be told what to do. And you don't escape responsibility just because *nobody told you that you had to do it*.

You can keep your head down and wait to be called on, or you can pay attention and ask yourself: "What am I going to do here to help my group?" That's how group decisions get implemented. That's how change happens. Be the change that you want for your group, for your community, for your world. Get busy, take ownership, and get things done.

INSIGHT: Your Decision's Impact on the Earth Community

Every group of decision makers is part of a larger group or larger community. Ultimately, we are all part of the great community called Earth.

I want what is best for my group, but which group? It is not OK for my local group to profit at the expense of my larger group—that simply shifts expenses to others. By the same token, doing what is best for my club is not OK if it hurts my town; doing what is best for my town is not OK if it hurts my country; and doing what is best for my country is not OK if it hurts the Earth community.

As your group makes decisions, consider the impact of those decisions on other groups and over time. Expand the circle of concern all the way to the Earth community and into the future. Decide things locally that will help the whole world. Decide things now that will help our kids and our kids' kids. To make good group decisions, we must resist the temptation to be guided entirely by local, short-term gain.

ATTITUDE #5: GOOD IN EVERYONE

Every person has something good to contribute to the group. If I write someone off because of how they look, I am limiting their contributions to future group decisions. Even if that person did something bad to me in the past, if I write them off, I am cutting off the opportunity of that person to give to the group and I am missing an opportunity to hear and incorporate their concerns.

Whether we like someone or not, if they are part of our group and if we are to make *good* group decisions together, we look for good things in that person. And we show respect at all times and in all situations.

INSIGHT: What Is a Show of Respect?

First, it's a show. A demonstration. It's visible, intended to get noticed. It's something a little out of the ordinary, on purpose. Like holding a door or bowing a head. It's visibly making an effort. A show of respect says: "This moment is special. I'm glad to be in it with you. Even if fleeting." Sometimes a show of respect happens in a flash, an eye-to-eye glance that says, "I believe in you."

One way to show respect is to get someone's name right. Or at least try. And that includes pronouns, last name, pronunciation, and maybe their title. Ask someone: "How would you like to be called?" Making these efforts says, "I'm trying to make friends with you." And as a practical matter, when we treat people with respect, they are more likely to bring forward their best self.

In my opinion, this attitude of *good in everyone* is at the core of the Quaker belief system and it's why I am a Quaker. George Fox, the founder of Quakerism, said, " . . . walk cheerfully over the world, answering that of God in everyone . . . "[14] If you walk around truly believing that God exists in every person, no matter how you define "God," you're far less likely to be mean to others

---

14 Journal of George Fox, 1891.

and far more likely to show respect to your fellows. Even when you have a really hard time believing that someone is good, acting *as if* they have good within them somewhere somehow will take you a long way toward positive outcomes.

To believe that there is *good in everyone* is to be antiracist. Many people believe that there are biological differences between races—that Black people are more athletic, that white people are more intellectual—that sort of thing. There aren't. Skin color, hair, and facial features are literally skin deep. Biologically there is no difference between me (a white guy) and a Black man, or a man of any other race. We are all human beings, the same species. When we believe in such differences—and I am absolutely guilty of such beliefs at times—it's called biological racism. We know today that there is no basis for it.[15]

The problem with thinking that different races of people have different abilities is that it's a half-step away from concluding that some races are better than others. It's precisely that belief—that my people are better than your people—that is responsible for almost all wars. It's a much better bet, morally and practically, to see all people of all races as equally worthy, as if there is good in each human being regardless of what they look like.

To make good group decisions we don't just "see" all people, we are proactive and deliberate and thoughtful about encouraging all people to participate. We provide accommodations and assistance as needed. We are especially welcoming and supportive of those who are usually on the fringes. We look up to all people and treat each person we meet with dignity and respect.

---

15 For more on this, see Vivian Chou, "How Science and Genetics are Reshaping the Race Debate of the 21st Century," Harvard University (blog), April 17, 2017, https://sitn.hms.harvard.edu/flash/2017/science-genetics-reshaping-race-debate-21st-century.

It's more than not being racist; it's being antiracist.[16] We deliberately learn about underprivileged cultures and history and terminology. And when we see someone treated bad just because of how they look, we do something about it. We speak up. We use whatever privilege we have to help the underprivileged have a voice. And even if we don't do these things because we believe there is God in every person, we are antiracist because we know there is good in every person, and the group is missing out on good stuff when people are shunned. Really. The practical benefits of inclusion are enormous.

THERE IS GOOD IN ME TOO

And this principle of good in everyone applies to me too. Whenever I refer to "everyone in the room," I'm in that room too. One of the helpful attitudes I bring into every meeting is "I am worthy." I am worthy of speaking up and I am worthy of volunteering to do tasks. When I really believe that there is good in me—good things from which the group can benefit—I speak up and I volunteer. I share the good things that I have to offer.

When I share the good in me, I serve as an example to others and serve as encouragement for them to dig deep and offer what's best in them. Good attitudes and good behaviors are contagious. They multiply. An attitude of *good in me* supports and encourages an attitude of *good in everyone*. As you are reading this, and when you are in a meeting, remember that there is good in you too.

On the other hand, if it's hard to see good in someone— if someone is always talking down about themselves or about

---

16 See *How to Be an Antiracist* by Ibram X. Kendi.

others or about the group and sees no value in contributing anything—that person does not need to be in a group trying to make good decisions. I am not saying that such a person with a bad attitude should be summarily kicked out of a group; I'm saying that such a person should be removed from *decision-making* for the group, either informally behind the scenes or formally in public view. Of course, *kicked out* seems like a harsh phrase. In actuality one might be eased out or gently persuaded or tactfully shown "a different job."

But sometimes a decision maker with a destructive attitude can't be removed. In such cases the other members of the group figure out a way to go around that person. Figure out how to get stuff done anyway. Try to contain the person's bad attitudes or actions in a box. One example is imposing time limits on how long somebody can speak in a meeting, so that person has to follow the time rule like everyone else. Be polite and respectful, and don't give them any reason to go on the offensive against you, but you also need to be strict in adhering to the time limit. Another tactic is to call for votes often so everyone can see that this person is in the minority over and over again. You can also not assign the person to any special teams, committees, or groups or give them any kind of job where they can have a destructive influence. And there's no need to be sneaky about any of these tactics. It's OK to say the reason: we need decision makers who believe in themselves and who believe in our group.

And again, don't overlook yourself. Sometimes we fall on hard times and become emotionally unstable or develop bad attitudes. When you recognize that in yourself, consider that maybe *you* should step out of decision-making for a bit. When you're not your best self, don't bring your bad stuff to the group.

INSIGHT: It's Better to Be Kind Than Right

The ego in me wants me to be right. The peace seeker in me wants me to be kind. The word *kind* is related to the word *kin*, meaning family. To be kind is to treat people like family, as if we were intimately connected over time.

To contribute to good group decisions, I feed the peace seeker within, keep the ego in check, and strive for kindness. I am more interested in developing healthy relationships with my fellow decision makers over the long term than I am in getting my way in the short term. I give unconditionally without expectation of return, free of strings. True kindness is both free and priceless.

* There is one exception: If you are oppressed or bullied, it's OK to fight back or stand up for yourself.

CHAPTER 5

Open to All Truths

WHEN I GO into group decision-making with a closed mind—thinking that I already know the answer—I might be standing in the way of good group decisions. For instance, I might think that my goal is to persuade the group that what I think is best; that my way is right. And if I am particularly persuasive or powerful, I might achieve my goal. But I will have missed the opportunity to make an even better decision than I could have imagined—because I closed off the opportunity to imagine it. Being open-minded is to truly accept that we don't know everything. It is to accept that we don't know most things, actually. And the things that we do know? We might be wrong.

Open-mindedness is an attitude of searching rather than of knowing, of learning rather than of telling. It is being non-judgmental and unprejudiced. It is being open to the possibility that you might learn something new from a person or a belief system that you don't like or have a bias against. It is being open to changing your mind based on new, good information from wherever it might come.

All groups—corporations, governments, whoever—make their worst decisions when they are stuck in their ways or guided by a single leader or small group of leaders who deliberately refuse to acknowledge new information. Bad group decisions happen when one or a few people are sure that they know what's best and close themselves off to even better possibilities.

The key to group sustainability is being open to new information and willing to make decisions and change behaviors based on that information. We know that those plant and animal species most able to adapt to changing environments are most likely to endure. Group cultures most able to adapt to changing circumstances are also most able to thrive.

When you're open-minded, you are not only open to new knowledge coming in, but also you are open to sharing knowledge and opinions with others. Your mind is open in both directions: you let stuff in and you let stuff out. The best group decision makers don't keep information to themselves as a means to gain power, and they don't withhold information to get their way. They freely share what they know and feel with other decision makers. In some groups you're actually supposed to share what's in your heart, no matter what it is.

Once, I was in a Quaker meeting when someone read a passage from the Pope's encyclical on the environment. I felt moved to speak up. I said some good things about the passage, but I also said, "There's one thing I can't agree with." The Pope's words basically said we must take responsibility for fixing the environment. I said out loud, "No, that's the problem. We should not be taking anything. It's not our responsibility to decide how to fix the environment. Let's get out of the way for a change, not always be taking from it and dumping in it and [air quotes] 'taking responsibility' for it. Let the environment lead. Let's follow for a change. Let's take responsibility for fixing ourselves so we are not so destructive to the environment." Something like that.

I had just challenged the Pope. In a church of sorts. Maybe I had offended some of my Quaker friends. Afterward I asked someone, "Did I say the right thing?" The response came without hesitation: "How could you not have? You spoke from your heart."

One extremely valuable contribution I can make to a group decision is to discern my own truths and share them with the group. Deep inside, what do I really feel? What do I really think? This requires me to cut through the clutter of whatever else is on my mind. Discerning my truth requires me to be honest with myself. It requires courage. It might make me feel vulnerable. It might unleash other truths that I didn't even plan on. Yet I am asked to be open to truths within, as well as truths coming at me from other places.

Open-mindedness also supports innovation and creativity. By being open to new ideas, being nonjudgmental, and sharing information, we maximize chances for creating breakthrough, leap-ahead ideas. Creativity is always the result of two or more ideas coming together. Innovation—truly creative solutions to group challenges—happens when we are open to the blending of all ideas, new and old, big and small, from anywhere or anyone.

Groups seeking truly creative decisions invite and make room for suggestions from all participants. When naturally dominant people are humble and when naturally shy people are courageous, prospects for good group decisions are dramatically increased.

If you have a strong opinion about something or recognize that you are dominating, consider that there might be a better way than yours; there might be better ideas out there worth hearing. The less you talk, the more you hear.

If you are part of a group where someone is dominating the conversation, speak up and say that you would like to hear from others. Appreciate and validate the dominant comments. Then move on. Say something like, "We appreciate your views but would like to hear other views also. Is there someone else who would like to weigh in on this?" In this way it's not about wanting to shut someone down, rather it's about wanting to hear from others.

Why Not a Street?

My cohousing group was planning the layout of the houses in the early stages of our site design. With the help of a landscape architect, we stood around a table with a map of our land and little Monopoly houses to help us imagine our neighborhood. We drew new lines on the map where the road might go and we moved the houses around. Imagining.

We were very close to deciding the location of our little model houses. They were all carefully placed on the outside of a ring-shaped road and all the houses faced a common area. We had made many decisions that led us to this point and we were about to finalize the plan.

Then somebody said, "Wait. Why a road? Why not a street?" The difference between a road and a street, the person explained, is that roads are rural and streets are urban. Roads have houses here and there, spread out, sometimes all on the same side like our design. Streets on the other hand are typically lined with houses on both sides looking across at each other. "If we are trying to design a community that will foster social interaction," the person explained, "why not a street?"

The new idea was difficult for many to swallow at first. A street? In the country? But because we were open, even at the last minute, we fully considered it. We talked it through and it seemed like a good idea. In the end (an hour later), we decided to make our community half road and half street. And that's how it is today. It works pretty great.

No one could have anticipated that particular solution but the stage had been set for magic to happen, for ideas to germinate that would grow into solutions.

GO AHEAD, CHANGE YOUR MIND

Leaders are often criticized for changing their minds on issues. I suppose it's because it indicates weakness, inconsistency, or lack of commitment to a particular doctrine. Sometimes it may indicate that the person is too easily subject to influence. But groups make their best decisions when every group member *is* subject to influence, when each one of us is open to hearing and acting on the wisdom of others and on new information.

Changing one's mind for trivial or self-serving reasons may indicate weakness, but changing one's mind in the face of new truths indicates growth and evolution. Actually, I want my leaders to change their minds based on new information. Know your values and morals well, but do not be so attached to them that they

I WANT MY LEADERS TO CHANGE THEIR MINDS BASED ON NEW INFORMATION

cause you to deny new truths. Be in touch with your beliefs, but also open to new information and new beliefs. One of the most powerful and helpful things one can say in a meeting is, "Well, I've changed my mind."

Also, don't let past experiences unreasonably limit your future decisions. When a past experience has forced you to "refuse to listen," it can limit the group. Be fully aware of the past, know your group's history, and remember the bad things that happened, but don't let an old idea dominate your mind. It's OK to glance in the rearview mirror but not be fixated. The wake of a boat has nothing to do with what the boat does in the future. The wake doesn't push the boat. The wake doesn't slow the boat. The wake doesn't steer the boat. A wake is only a trail left behind. Look ahead and point the boat wherever you want.

Phrases such as "We've never done it that way before" or "Tried that; didn't work" presume that just because something happened a certain way in the past, something else can't happen in the future. We often invoke this illusion because it is comforting, secure, and less risky. It gives us a very handy excuse for not trying new things and keeps us close to the familiar— whether good or bad. The illusion limits our choices, and actually there's a lot of comfort in limited choices. Full freedom is scary. But to make good group decisions in the future, we are asked to make peace with the past. We are asked to forgive, accept, and let go so we can move forward with the full array of choices before us.

Traditions Can Change

We have a shipbuilding company here in Maine called Bath Iron Works. They build warships for the United States Navy, and every time they launch one, two or three times a year, it's kind of a big deal. Our federal senators and/or representatives are usually present or maybe the governor. The company slides the ship down into the water, a well-known dignitary breaks a bottle of champagne over the bow, and everyone wishes the ship good luck as it begins its service in the Navy. It's been typical at these ceremonies to release a bunch of helium balloons. What fun! The celebrities are on the platform, the bottle of champagne gets cracked against the steel hull, and hundreds of balloons are released. Up and down the coast we can all see that another ship has been launched.

I used to work for the Maine State Planning Office where we had a program aimed at reducing marine debris—garbage in the ocean. When you let go of hundreds of balloons near the ocean, you can bet a lot of them are going to end up as garbage in the water and pose a real risk to wildlife and human health. We had a good relationship with the person at the shipyard who coordinated these events and who was in charge of their public relations. We asked if they would stop releasing the balloons as part of the ceremony. It was important for the shipyard to uphold tradition, he explained, and he resisted our requests. Ships continued to get launched with balloon releases. But you know what? He changed his mind. After a while—after being presented with compelling data—he could see that stopping the balloon releases was the right thing to do and so he changed his mind. He had to persuade lots of other people at the shipyard and even the congressional leaders and the Navy that the old tradition would need to change. They were open to it. This is how progress happens.

SAYING *I DON'T KNOW* IS SUPER HELPFUL

The most helpful comment someone can make in a group is usually *not* "I know what we should do." Instead, the most helpful comment is usually "I don't know what we should do." An attitude of "I don't know" is often more helpful than "I know it all."

Some people feel compelled to put

IF YOU DON'T KNOW WHAT YOU'RE TALKING ABOUT, STOP TALKING.

up false fronts driven by ego or pride. They may be so nervous about being exposed for not knowing something that they would rather act as though they are not in doubt—even though they may be wrong, even frequently wrong. This is a big problem in group decision-making because it causes inefficiencies and it destroys trust. When someone really doesn't know an answer to something and they make something up—when they show off with their speculations—it wastes everyone's time and often sends people down a rabbit trail or off in the wrong direction.

It's really simple. If you don't know what you're talking about, stop talking. If you are trying to get me to do something I don't want to do or if you are trying to get something from me, then I understand that you would feel justified in making stuff up or bending truths. But if you are my partner in trying to make a decision that's best for all of us, stop with the hot air and listen to people who know stuff.

With an attitude of accepting that we don't understand but *want* to understand, we are an open mind waiting to be filled with information. When I am waiting to learn from others rather than waiting to tell others, I have an exponentially better chance of hearing new perspectives, feeling new emotions, and gaining true understanding about the world around me. When I am part of a group of decision makers who want to fully understand an issue before deciding on it, we have an exponentially better chance of making a good group decision.

Another challenge to open-mindedness, in addition to not wanting to look like I don't have answers, is impatience. There's almost always a sense that something needs to be decided or done right away and so we make fast decisions and charge forward even though we know full well that we have not looked very hard for the best solution. And in a production culture such as the United States, no one wants to hold up progress. Better to make a bad decision fast than a good decision slow. Unfortunately, this is often the way.

Ideally, we want to keep our minds open until understanding emerges. And if understanding doesn't emerge, we should not move hastily on to a subsequent step of deciding. We should not pretend to understand just so we can move quickly (perhaps recklessly) to the next step.

There's a popular quote often attributed to Carl Jung: "Thinking is difficult, that's why most people judge." It's way easier to assume things about other people than to try and understand them. This is why it is way easier to make conflict than peace, and way easier to make bad group decisions than good group decisions.

SAY NO TO SUNK COSTS

Let's consider a group that is heading down a path of building a new factory when suddenly the direction gets questioned. The land has been bought. The soils have been tested, the site plan has been approved, and an architect is under contract and has begun work. A huge amount of money and effort has gone into planning and preparing for the new facility. Then a new piece of land goes up for sale nearby—a better piece of land—and someone raises a new idea that perhaps the factory would be better located there instead. A very compelling argument is made that the new property would be much better over the long run. Yet some people argue, "No, we should stay on track with the plan because we have invested so much money in it already."

Just because a group has invested money or time in the past is never a valid reason for limiting choices in the future. Economists call these *sunk costs*; they are gone and cannot be retrieved. Sunk costs are never a justification for spending more time and effort on what may be a bad decision. No sense pouring good money after bad.

Or let's say you're moving into a new house where the previous owners invested a great deal of money in a game room with a pool table, a dartboard, and a bar. But you don't know how to play pool or darts, and you don't drink. You are allowed to rip out the previous owner's investment. Those decisions were made at another time in other circumstances. You need to make the best decision for you and your family going forward, regardless of past investments or choices.

Groups move into new rooms and new buildings and new situations every day. Conditions around us are ever-changing. Every moment can be the start of something fresh and new and need not carry the baggage of the past.

GRAB A POSITIVE OUTLOOK
AND HEAD FOR ADVENTURE

I was once on a ropes course strapped into a safety harness and instructed to walk across a tightrope fifty feet off the ground. Even with another rope to hang on to higher up, it took balance and courage to attempt the exercise. Several people in my group opted out (no one was forced to do something they didn't want to do). I wondered if I should risk it or not.

I saw the guy before me step out onto the rope, and I saw him struggle. The rope wobbled back and forth, and he fought for every step. As I watched him, a thought came to me—just slipped quietly in as a whisper at first: "I can do this." What a wonderful thought! Whenever positive thoughts pass through our heads, we have to grab them and quickly weave them into our imaginations.

A positive attitude means taking every opportunity to improve our image of ourselves, our group, and the future. It doesn't mean that we are in denial about bad things or that we can't have poor opinions of certain ideas, situations, or people. It doesn't mean we don't have fears. But what it does mean is that no matter the idea, situation, or person, we are open to positive outcomes; we allow ourselves to imagine them.

People who are not positive are generally fearful of the future and are unable to trust that things will turn out fine. Such attitudes can suck passion and enthusiasm from your group. On the other hand, people with a can-do attitude don't get paralyzed by fear and they are willing to take steps forward even without knowing where they will lead. They're able to see and describe and act out visions of change for the better. Attitudes of optimism, humility, willingness to cooperate, and openness to change make for an adventurous road to good group decisions.

As I stepped up to the little platform to start across the tight-rope, I said over and over, almost as a meditation: "I can do this. I can do this." In my heart, the idea built from a whisper to a shout, and I had to repeat it to myself several times as I made it across the rope. And though I had to stop as I felt my breathing and my heart pounding, I was able to recharge my vision of myself actually making the crossing. And I made it!

If a group member predicts negativity, it can contribute to negative things actually occurring. If someone spreads the word that "it's gonna be bad," it actually increases the chances that "it's gonna be bad." So if you speculate, speculate about good things. And just because you can't see a good outcome doesn't mean that one isn't waiting for you.

In a group setting, having a positive outlook is to believe in and work for positive outcomes. With a positive attitude, we smile. We laugh. We are upbeat and spread good cheer. We shine light on things. We don't deny or ignore darkness, but we are careful not to spread it or grow it.

We don't need to believe that everything is possible all the time. That's not realistic or practical. And we need to accept that people have different dispositions, different hormone balances, different temperaments. Some people struggle greatly to be pos-itive. It can't be turned on and off like a switch. We need to be tolerant of those who suffer from depression or anxiety. What's important is to try not to label things lightly or as categorically impossible. Closing off possibilities stifles creativity and limits our chances of making good group decisions.

As a meeting facilitator and leader, I do lots of things to encourage positivity. When I invite someone to a meeting whether verbally or in writing, I try to convey excitement and optimism. At the start of the meeting, as people come into the meeting room or onto the screen, I greet them with a smile and a positive attitude. If there's any kind of warm-up activity, you can be sure it's slanted toward positivity and gratitude. And I remind the group periodically through the meeting what we've accomplished. Oh, and this too: Before every meeting (except when I forget sometimes), I say a little prayer asking for help in making it a positive and peaceful experience. Whether you believe in God or not, pausing to think such a thought has the practical benefit of setting an intention.

Where we look is what we see. When we focus on solutions, the solutions get bigger. When we focus on problems, the problems get bigger. If we look for negative things, we will find them. If we look for positive things, we will find them.

Take an example from our canine friends. When two dogs approach each other with wagging tails, the outcome is almost always good. When one or more dogs are barking, it is hard to know what will happen. Approach people wagging your tail, expecting good things, and letting your optimism show. Perhaps you have seen the bumper sticker: Wag more. Bark less.

INSIGHT: Positive Feedback Is Like Rocket Fuel

If you agree with what someone is saying or like what someone is doing, the best way to get them to say or do more of it is to provide positive feedback. Tell them. It doesn't have to be with fanfare or fireworks, or even written or spoken; a nod or a smile can ignite forward momentum. Positive feedback is like rocket fuel. It propels one forward in the direction already headed.

We can't expect someone to say or do positive things in the absence of feedback. It's very inefficient to expect someone to figure

continued

out, with zero feedback, what would meet our approval. Want efficiency and stellar performance? Provide positive feedback. Rather
than walk around and try to catch someone doing something wrong,
walk around and try to catch someone doing something right. And
tell them. In front of others.

TO BE PATIENT IS TO BE OK WITH MESSINESS

Impatience can get in the way of making good group decisions.
If we value the work we are doing, we have to take the time to do
it right. Discrete decisions about little things seem tiny but they
add up to great creations. It might seem to take a long time for a
spring bulb to bloom, but once it does the result is magnificent.
Same with a tree or a forest or a river valley. Like nature, if we
want magnificent results we need to practice patience. Give time
for new paths to open up. An attitude of patience allows good
group decisions to grow.

We often lose patience with group decision-making processes
because they seem to take too long and seem too involved or
unclear. We often judge decisions by how long they take to make
rather than by the results of their implementation. We often want
fast decisions at the expense of good decisions. This is why we
often rush to make a decision even if it's not the best one, just for
the comfort of having it decided. Because we can't stand the anxiety and conflict of the process, we just get it over with. Yet a big
decision that will affect lots of people for a long time *should* cause
anxiety and conflict. We should take significant time to make
significant decisions. If short-term disorder (decisions in limbo
and unable to move forward) must be endured for long-term
peace (much more likely if a good decision is made), so be it.

Rushed decisions made by groups also can have significant

negative consequences. Many are irreversible. Bad decisions often require arduous decisions later to correct previous errors. Better to invest days, weeks, and months in a good decision than to live with bad outcomes for years, decades, and centuries.

IF WE ARE MOVING IN THE RIGHT DIRECTION, WE MIGHT GET THERE.

Confucius said, "Do not be desirous of having things done quickly. Do not look at small advantages . . . Looking at small advantages prevents great affairs from being accomplished."[17] Many of us have been told, "Don't just sit there; do something!" But when we are open-minded and patient we might better say, "Don't just do something; sit there!" Good group decision-makers are not as concerned with how fast they are moving as they are with moving in the right direction. If we are moving in the right direction, we might get there. If we are moving fast but in the wrong direction, it just means we will get to the wrong place faster. If you think making good group decisions is inefficient, making bad group decisions is even more inefficient.

Don't Decide Too Quickly

My cohousing community spent months designing our common house. It's at the center of our community and includes a large kitchen, a gathering space, and other common areas. And we have some weirdly placed walking paths near the common house, some that no one uses.

As a group we made a number of decisions guided by an architect who was familiar both with designing common houses and

continued

17 Confucius, The Confucian Analects, the Great Learning & the Doctrine of the Mean.

working with groups. Oh my gosh, so many long-lasting decisions have to be made when you are designing and building a house! How you are going to use the space, how the space should be arranged, how much money you should spend and on what, and how it should look in the end. Because we were designing a common house, all those decisions were made in common.

Just when we had made a big bunch of important decisions about the house design, along came another bundle of decisions. Landscaping! Where to put the trees, the bushes, the garden beds? Where to put the walking paths?

I'm not sure just how it happened, but many months later, as the building was nearing completion, some bulldozers showed up and some walking paths appeared. These were not wimpy foot-wide trails, but substantial wide walkways made with roadbed material.

"But wait a minute," said Enid in a general meeting weeks later. Enid was an especially practical member of our community. "Why are the paths *here*?" she asked. The best answer anyone could provide was something about a decision having to be made in a hurry so someone standing in the town office took out a pen and drew paths on our site plan moments before it was submitted to the Town. That was a bad group decision. The paths are in stupid places.

We should have planned for no paths at all until the common house was built and until we had lived with it for a while to see where the natural paths emerged, even if it was more costly to bring the bulldozers back later. But someone couldn't stand to leave that detail undone at the time of planning, couldn't stand the untidiness of a landscape plan with no paths. And for the rest of us, we were too weary to notice or make a thing of it at the time.

This is a small example of a footpath in a wrong place. Not too big a deal. We have to live with this or pay to have it fixed. But this dynamic happens a lot in groups—and sometimes with extremely high costs. Certain members rush to decide every last detail just for the satisfaction of deciding every last detail, no matter if those decisions are good or not. It happens when we design houses and it happens when we design laws.

I had a friend who would say with peaceful acceptance, "There will be dirty dishes in the sink on the day that I die." Things are always in progress. No decision is ever complete and final anyway, so decide only as much as you have to. It's OK to leave things unfinished. Nature, our supreme example, is always unfinished.

CHAPTER 6

No One Is Smarter Than All of Us

I ONCE RAN a meeting in a corporate headquarters for a manufacturing company. It was a very typical corporate office in a landscaped industrial park. The lobby and entrance area was pretty stark; it gave the impression of a company that prides itself on saving money—no pomp and circumstance or trying to be flashy in any way. I was led down a long hallway carrying my projector and equipment to set up for a meeting. I was wearing a suit and tie for this one. I've worked with many corporate clients, but it's not really my thing to be in that atmosphere day in and day out. So it was different for me, and I felt a little out of place.

Until I was shown into the meeting room. At first it seemed very stark and minimalist. They hadn't spent money on their corporate boardroom either. In fact, there were no paintings on the wall or adornments of any kind, except one sign. It was framed and it said, "No one in this room is smarter than all of us." I knew instantly that I was in a good place.

For me this quote embodies the concept of both humility and inclusion. It says "I don't know what's best" and "I want to hear from you." It's a magic combination for making truly innovative and creative decisions. "No one is smarter" is the humility part of the phrase. That's addressed in the next chapter: Authentic Effort Builds Trust. "Than all of us": that's the inclusion part. To actually be sure we are making the best possible decision available to us, we want to hear from *all* of those who will be affected.

Although it may be difficult at times, we must allow people to be different, expressive, creative, and weird. "Each of us has a piece of the truth," and if your piece looks weird or even threatening to me, so be it. If it's your truth we want to hear it. We encourage it, in fact. To make good group decisions we encourage each participant to listen to the drumbeat within them and share their dance with us, whatever it sounds or looks like. We are open to new ideas from anywhere. We deliberately include and encourage participation of people and perspectives that are traditionally marginalized. We help the quiet person step into the light and shine.

When the loudest, wealthiest voices prevail and don't give quieter, less-privileged voices a chance to be heard, we won't achieve unison and people will feel disgruntled. Further, the group won't be considering all the angles, any unintended consequences, or any wild and creative ideas. For those who are accustomed to being the loudest and the most influential, it's hard to let go and really consider alternative ways of looking at things and doing things, but the payoff is almost always worth it.

I was once hired to work with a state agency that wanted to build a website to provide health care cost information to the general public. The agency director and board had ideas for how this website should look and feel. Yet they went an extra step and formed a consumer advisory council to hear perspectives different from their own. On this council were some older people, some disabled people, and some people with different skin colors, and the agency director worked hard to take the advice of these people. In the end the agency made a much better website because the director and board listened to viewpoints different from their own. The project took more effort and it was a little uncomfortable. The leaders had to make changes to their vision that were inconvenient. But they achieved buy-in from a broad range of consumers and they also made a website that would be more widely appealing in the end.

"One might ponder whether America's gift to the world has been democracy or perhaps capitalism or perhaps even baseball." I once heard someone begin a keynote speech this way. "America's gift to the world is diversity," the speaker declared.[18] We have a lot of American principles based on the notion that we are better because of our diversity, yet we are not very good at practicing them most of the time. I think we have the collective sense that we are a better people, a better nation, because we encourage all voices and different opinions. We love our right to free speech, and we love to talk about giving everyone a voice,

18 Ed McMahon, Senior Resident Fellow, Urban Land Institute, at the Maine Downtown Center Annual Conference, 1999.

yet we easily slide into listening to the most traditional, the loudest, the wealthiest among us. We easily slide into placing barriers in front of our opponents like voter suppression and gerrymandering. When we stand on a pedestal of what we think we know best, we easily forget the magic that comes with true diversity.

LOVE AND FORGIVENESS
FUEL GOOD DECISIONS

Most group decision-making models don't mention love. When making decisions on behalf of others, we're supposed to be objective, rational, and unemotional. It's kind of an unwritten rule that we're not supposed to let emotions interfere with high-stakes decisions. This may work well on the field of battle where the goal is to beat the other guy. But it doesn't work well when we are trying to find win-win, peaceful solutions.

Including love in group decisions means encouraging passion and compassion. It means treating everyone as a valued contributor and no one as an enemy. It means making decisions not just with your head, but also with your heart. When

FORGIVENESS IS NOT TO DENY THAT A BAD DEED WAS DONE; IT'S TO HELP YOU PREVENT A BAD PAST FROM MAKING A BAD FUTURE.

I served as board chair of a private Waldorf school for students in kindergarten through high school, I saw the teachers begin many meetings—actually every meeting—with a verse, a meditation, a song, or a poem, and a deliberate intention to invite love into the decision-making process. Quakers also start their business meetings with reverence; it's called "waiting worship." We are simply giving love a chance to be present among us.

In principle, it is love that truly changes hearts and transforms people, not power or rules. It is love that compels sustained changes in behavior, not oaths or doctrines. It is love that provides a willingness to give, and it is love that helps us accept, let go, and find peace.

In addition to looking forward with love, we can also look backward with love. That's called forgiveness. It's when you look back on a bad deed with love and acceptance. Forgiveness is not to deny that a bad deed was done; it's to help you prevent a bad past from making a bad future.

If I have an altercation with somebody and I walk away thinking that I have been wronged, I have a choice. I can carry around that resentment and let it cloud every future transaction I have with that person. I can let it be a wedge of avoidance between me and my adversary, or a club of conflict. Yet if I'm able to genuinely forgive, I can greet that person with a smile and work productively with them. If I'm able to forgive, it drains the resentment out of my body and gives me freedom to think and move in new positive ways. I can still believe that I was wronged, deeply wronged, yet I can make a choice to not let that bog me down.

Forgiveness begins with a decision. Sometimes the most we can do is to *decide* we will at least try to forgive. Even to get to the point of that decision—to try to forgive—takes practice. It can be really hard. Yet it *can* be practiced. It *is* a choice to try. If you can do it, it will bring freedom and peace.

It's Not Their Fault. It's Their Type.

We each have a personality type hardwired into us, and it's not likely to change. There are many methods of assessing personality types. The Myers-Briggs Type Indicator is the most popular among them. Categorizing people into basic types has been going on since about 400 BC. Hippocrates called them the four humors: sanguine (cheerful), melancholic (pensive), phlegmatic (calm), and choleric (fiery).

Specific personality types come with specific personality traits. Our personal types indicate how we learn, how we act, how we perceive others and the world, and how some abilities come naturally to us and some don't.

In a group decision meeting, we want to provide opportunities for everyone to participate equally and optimally, each in a way that fits with their own personality style. As a group facilitator I might collect ideas by asking for raised hands or shoutouts, and that's easiest for some types: the extroverts. But if I want to include everyone, I could also collect ideas in writing some-how. For instance: "Take a minute and write your reactions to this question or this thought . . . take two minutes . . . " There can be a lot of variations on how people might write things in a meeting: Paraphrase your idea into a headline and put it on a big sticky note on the wall. Type it into a chatbot or an online document. After individual writing, talk with one or two people and share your ideas. Slower reflective processes generate more contribu-tions from introverts.

When someone doesn't do something the way I would do it, I try to keep in mind that it's probably not their intention to be difficult; it's just that we are not the same types of people. We cannot help that I view the world differently and solve problems

differently. Our differences are not our fault. As a practical matter, it works really well to see other peoples' differences not as
faults or problems or challenges at all, but as their gifts.

AN ATTITUDE OF GRATITUDE

When we have a positive attitude and look forward, we see a
bright future. When we have a positive attitude and look backward, that's called gratitude. If I have something to complain
about, I'm going to have a hard time contributing positively to
good group decisions, or I may even be unable to move forward
with the group. Gratitude is like traction. Without it, we can slip
and slide and get bogged down in self-pity, anger, resentment, or
whatever negative emotion is pulling on us. With a grateful view
of the past, we have a good footing to take us forward.

Sometimes people are unhappy because there is a difference
between what they have and what they want—or *think* they
want. I call this the *gap of discontent*. And in American culture we
are incessantly told that the cure for the gap of discontent is to
acquire more. Get more stuff and you'll close the gap! Advertisers
incessantly tell us that buying more products and services will
lead to happiness.

Yet there is another way to erase the difference between *want*
and *have*, a better way to happiness. You can change your attitude
about what you have by deciding to be happier with what you
have. Really. That's what gratitude is. It is finding joy in what we
already have within us and around us. Gratitude lessens our need
for more or different. It helps us find peace.

5. HOW TO CLOSE THE GAP OF DISCONTENT

OPTION A
Change what I have

OPTION B
Change what I want

WHAT I WANT

**GAP OF
DISCONTENT**

Get more stuff

Feel more gratitude

WHAT I HAVE

I'm **unhappy** when there's a gap between what I want and what I have.
There are two ways to close that gap and get **happy**.

When I have a grateful attitude, I bring assets to my group. For one thing, I am in a position to give. I have assets in the bank. When I have a resentful attitude, I'm more disposed to want to take. If I'm feeling down or underserved or if I feel resentful toward the world or the people around me, I might be thinking of ways to get my share. My mindset is on how to get. I am driven by self-interest. When I have an attitude of gratitude—simply aware of my blessings and the good things in my life—I am more inclined toward giving. For one thing, I don't feel so needy for additional things. For another thing, I want others to have this good feeling that I have. I want others to be need-free. When I have genuine gratitude, it's actually fun to give stuff away.

Having an attitude of gratitude is always a choice. It's not always easy but always possible. When we feel down about the state of the environment or the political divisiveness in the United States, it helps to seek out goodness and to discover things that other people are doing to address both. Finding good in others is inspirational, and it replaces a sense of resignation with a sense of possibility. When you see you are not alone, you feel energized. We can decide to think in a certain way. We can decide to focus on the good things within us and around us. We can persuade ourselves that what we have is enough, or even that what we have is really terrific.

NOT FROM THE MIND OF ONE PERSON

The best group solution is unlikely to ever come from the head of one person. Usually there's an illusion. A single person makes a statement, and we all say, "Aha, that's it! That's what's best for the group!" But before the thought came out of that person, a whole lot of stuff went into that head. A lot of stuff was shared from other people. A lot of truths were shared and blended together to help make a good solution for the group as a whole.

When I'm trying to make a decision by myself, I can imagine great solutions. But when I invite the ideas of people who think differently than me, people who have had different experiences than I have had, when I invite their imaginations into the conversation, we will come up with solutions beyond my wildest imagination. We each have different experiences, different truths, and when we put all those different truths together, we are most likely to arrive at a decision that's best for the group as a whole.

Whose Idea Was That Anyway?

It was the second board meeting of a newly formed nonprofit—a farm that would grow organic food for food banks and pantries. I was on the board and we worked in small groups on what to call the organization. We didn't start with names but with concepts. We threw out words that we wanted the name to convey. Feelings. Images. After a while one of the board members, Amy, blurted out "growing to give." Those of us in Amy's little group knew immediately it was a good name. When the whole board heard the words, everyone knew we had a winner. And that phrase became the nonprofit's name.

I actually watched Amy form the words in her head and say them one at a time, in order. She said the words, but I have never once heard her take credit for the name. Another super-helpful practice is to give ideas to the group without ownership. Let the group trash your idea or change your idea or adopt your idea. It matters not to the good group giver. I think Amy would say that the name came from a process that she simply leaned into and in which she did her part. There were lots of parts. For instance, founders John and Patty designed and pushed us through a deliberate naming process in hopes of germinating a great idea. And it worked.

CHAPTER 7

Authentic Effort
Builds Trust

"DECISIONS ARE MADE by those who show up."[19] Producer
Aaron Sorkin wrote those words for his character, President Josiah
Bartlet, in *The West Wing*. But showing up means more than just
putting ourselves physically in the meeting room. It's about being
present mentally and emotionally too. If we are distracted by things
from the past (reflecting or "stewing" about what happened this
morning) or things that might happen in the future (daydreaming
or worrying about tomorrow), we are not fully present. If we are
distracted by something else going on at the same time but in a
different place (thinking about our kid in the daycare room next
door rather than paying attention to the speaker), we are not fully

----

19 Aaron Sorkin, Producer, "What Kind of Day Has It Been," *The West Wing*.

present. If we are in two conversations at once—maybe one on social media and one in person—we are not fully present for either.

When we are not fully present, we are likely making a poor investment of our time and energy. Since we're not putting our all into it, our chances of creating new and positive things are lower. The Buddha has said: "Do not dwell in the past, do not dream of the future, concentrate the mind on the present moment."[20]

But being present and free from distraction is a lot more than simply showing up and paying attention. It means being prepared in advance—in what I call a "spiritual" sense. It means that when we come to meetings—

- We're not angry. We're not fearful. Ideally, we aren't tired or in a bad mood.

- We are open-minded and not attached to certain expectations. One trick I do is to imagine worst outcome and then imagine myself accepting that. This helps me be open-minded.

- We're optimistic and look forward to seeing good things in people and in the situations around us.

- We're not unreasonably distracted by other things that are happening, have happened, or that might happen in our lives.

- We're alert, clear-headed, balanced, and spiritually prepared.

---

20 This quote is often attributed to Buddha from *The Teaching of Buddha: The Buddhist Bible: A Compendium of Many Scriptures Translated from the Japanese*, published in 1934 by The Federation of All Young Buddhist Associations of Japan. Yet there is debate over how the original words should be translated. For more on this see: https://fakebuddhaquotes.com/do-not-dwell-in-the-past-do-not-dream-of-the-future.

INSIGHT: Keep Expectations in Check

In any group endeavor we have expectations of others. If these expectations don't pan out, it often leads to resentment and discontent, which can lead to conflict. The surest way to avoid resentment is to keep your expectations low, of yourself and others.

Avoid false expectations. Expect from people only what they have specifically agreed to and even then, keep in mind that most people are not capable of doing all that they agree to. Don't expect too much.

Sometimes I find myself a victim of my own expectations. No one actually agreed to do a particular thing, but in my head, I expected it to happen. Then when it doesn't happen, I get angry, probably angry at others. Yet the fault is not with them but with me. The moment I committed my fault was when I set the false expectation in my head.

BE AUTHENTIC

Something is authentic if it really is what it presents to be. A person is authentic if their inner beliefs are aligned with their outer actions. An easy way to judge a person's authenticity is to see if they are consistent in different settings. Am I the same person with one group of people as I am with another? Do I say one thing in public but then act differently when no one is looking?

When I lived in England as a boy many years ago, a derogatory term that we called each other was *poser*. "Oh, that guy is such a poser! I can't stand him." That meant that the person was consumed with trying to be someone he wasn't. He tried to wear clothes that were out of his league and talk in ways that simply weren't genuine. And he didn't pull it off very well.

A PERSON IS AUTHENTIC IF THEIR INNER BELIEFS ARE ALIGNED WITH THEIR OUTER ACTIONS.

Do you want to pull off a certain persona and expect people to really believe it over a long time? Then be authentic. "Be yourself; everyone else is already taken."[21] The surest way to present a consistent and trustworthy persona is for all your actions to come from a consistent place, deep within *you*. Some people don't want to show their inner selves because they intentionally want to deceive. Others think it's OK to hide truths or present false truths in order to gain an upper hand. Some people may not view members of the group as being in this together but rather in competition with each other, and thus, in order to win, it's OK to deceive.

An attitude of "it's OK to deceive my opponent to get my way" is a hugely inefficient way for a group to try to make decisions together. Plus, it's dangerous. When people don't put all their cards on the table (even if they think they have a bad hand and don't want to show it), the group ends up making decisions based on incomplete information, and those decisions are highly likely to miss the mark.

One reason people resist showing their inner selves is because the group culture around them makes them feel unworthy or that their contributions are not valued. Perhaps the culture is oppressive or bullying. In some cultures, people can't or don't want to show any type of vulnerability. It's hard to be authentic in groups

---

21 Widely attributed to Oscar Wilde yet there is no evidence that he said it. Apparently.

with such a culture, unless your own values and beliefs are in lockstep with the group values and beliefs and then it's a dream come true.

Another reason people don't show their inner selves is because they don't *know* their inner selves. It's not that they want to be deceitful. It's not that they are embarrassed to share their true feelings and beliefs. It's that they're not sure what their true feelings and beliefs are. This happens a lot. And we usually try to hide it. Yet this is a legitimate reason and the group needs to be patient with such people. If you're the one who doesn't know what you think, that's fine. For a while. Yet at some point the group needs to move along even if one or more members "aren't sure." When I'm in that "not sure" category for too long, I let go and trust my fellows; I trust those who do have clarity. I don't let my unsureness hold up the group.

For my words and deeds to be consistently aligned with my inner truth, I first need to know my inner truth. I need to know what I believe and what I stand for. This is hard for some people. Knowing inner truth means we are in touch with ourselves and with what is really in our hearts. Some people are unable to speak truth because they cannot figure out what it is within themselves. And sometimes truths change within ourselves and in others due to new circumstances or new knowledge.

To be authentic you have to decide that you want to be authentic, that you don't want to intentionally deceive others. It is a decision to put community first, to put we over *me*. But being authentic is more than just a decision. It's real work. Self-work. Personal growth and development. Being authentic is gaining the self-esteem and courage to put yourself out there. It is continually seeking what's true for you and what isn't and continually acting on your inner truth. It is continually asking, "Who am I?" and always acting accordingly.

INSIGHT: Know When Not to Speak

Just because I think something doesn't mean I have to say it or act on it. My first thought may not be my best. Often, my first thought may be an absurd one and serve to warn me how *not* to react.

Sharing first thoughts can be deeply counterproductive to good group decisions. Like first brush strokes on a canvas, first thoughts provide a starting place for more refined thoughts, for subsequent brush strokes. The painting is not ready to show.

When we share first thoughts, we run a substantial risk of offending others, saying things we will regret, and requiring the group to spend time on issues that turn out to be a waste of time. Best to sit with our thoughts until a clear picture emerges of what we want to say.

BE TRUSTWORTHY

Research by Jim Kouzes and Barry Posner found that a leader's most desired quality is credibility. They write in their book, *The Leadership Challenge*, "It's clear that if we're willing to follow someone . . . we first want to assure ourselves that the person is worthy of our trust."[22]

Being trustworthy doesn't happen by saying "trust me." It

---

22 Jim Kouzes and Barry Posner, *The Leadership Challenge: How to Make Extraordinary Things Happen in Organizations* (Jossey-Bass, 2017).

happens when people see alignment between someone's words and their deeds—their authenticity. The quickest way to build trust with someone is to say what you are going to do and do it. Demonstrate that you can be trusted to follow through. The quickest way to erode trust is to say you will do something and then not do it.

We've all seen somebody come into a new job or a new role and promise great things but then not follow up on them. But it's not just over-promising that erodes credibility and erodes

THE QUICKEST WAY TO BUILD TRUST WITH SOMEONE IS TO SAY WHAT YOU ARE GOING TO DO AND DO IT.

trust; it's also inconsistency. Think about a leader who praises one person for completing a task but not someone else who does the same thing. Or the leader who follows through on certain things but not on others. We've all seen that, and it causes us to mistrust that person.

The way we discern truth is by looking at something from multiple angles. We ask several people for their versions of the truth and we look for commonalities. It's similar with trust. If I look at a person's behavior from several different angles, in different settings and with different people, a picture emerges of the person's trustworthiness.

When someone doesn't do what they say, we usually assume it was a breakdown in the *doing*. We might be inclined to think, "He didn't follow through again!" But often, the breakdown was in the *saying*. It might be more appropriate to think, "It's not his fault for being unable to follow through. He knows he can't complete a task like that. He shouldn't have *said* he could in the first place."

It's easier to say things than do things. This is why we say things that we do not mean. And this is how we lose credibility.

We say things that will make things easy and make people happy in the short run. But in the long run, when we don't deliver on our words, our credibility suffers.

Show Your Beliefs Where People Can See

In Quaker Meeting on June 26, 2016, in the old Meetinghouse down the road from my house, Dorothy Selebwa, director of the Kakamega Orphans Care Centre in Kenya, told this story:

An African Quaker woman was walking on a long journey alone. As night approached, she was very tired and needed to rest but didn't know anyone in the area. She came across some children playing soccer. She called a young boy over. "Would you come here, please?" the tired woman asked.

The boy came bounding up and she spoke kindly to him. "May I know your name?" After he said his name, the woman asked, "Do you know of any Quaker women in the area? I have walked a long way and I am tired. Night is approaching."

"Why yes, actually," the boy replied cheerfully. "I do. Would you like me to take you?"

"Yes," the woman said smiling. And the boy took her arm and led her slowly to the village. They walked by other children playing and walked past houses and right past the boy's own house to the next house and knocked on the door.

When a woman answered the door, the boy said, "This traveling woman has asked to meet a Quaker woman. She is on a journey walking alone and she is very tired and night is approaching." The homeowner invited the traveler in and the boy ran off. The woman cooked dinner for the traveler and made a bed for her and they said a

Quaker prayer before sleep. In the morning the two women ate breakfast together before the traveling woman departed, very grateful.

The boy told his mother, "I met a traveling woman who wanted to meet a Quaker woman, so I took her next door."

"Why next door?" the mother replied, startled. "I am a Quaker woman."

"You are?" The boy replied. "Momma, I have seen you yell at father and I have seen you quarrel with the neighbors and I have seen you hate people. I'm sorry, Momma, I didn't know you were a Quaker."

The boy's mother had been raised learning Quaker values. But she didn't *do* Quaker values. Actions speak louder than words. We listen more to what people do than what people say. And it is people doing things, rather than saying things and believing things and wishing things, that gets stuff done.

Whenever I notice that I am about to agree to something, I take a breath. At the very least, I acknowledge I am making some sort of commitment; my debt will be called at a future time. I take a moment and realize what I am agreeing to. I give myself a moment to ponder. Sometimes just a crack of quiet space is enough for some truth to sneak into my thinking. If it is a big decision, I sleep on it. Before I say, "I'll serve on the committee," or "I'll get that," or "I'll do that," I really consider what follow-through will look like. I imagine how it will be.

And saying no is OK. Often, saying no is the very best thing for all concerned. A quick and solid no is far better in the long run than half-hearted, stalling, or hollow yes. If your no stands on solid ground then make it known with no fuzziness. That helps everyone.

Building trust is not just "the right thing to do"; trust has enormous practical implications for group decision-making. To be trustworthy is to carry an attitude that I'm not going to say things lightly or make promises lightly. It is an attitude of "I can be counted on." It is an attitude that is critical for good group decisions.

Origins of the word *trust* date back to around 1200 and the Old Norse word for "rely on, make strong and safe." I trust my climbing rope will hold my weight, that the lights will come on when I flip the switch, that my kids will be safe in the house alone, and that my health care workers will know what they're doing.

Trust breeds efficiency. When expectations are broken—someone says one thing in a meeting but does another afterward—it makes for terrible inefficiencies. Gathering information for decision-making becomes a huge challenge when there is no open sharing or there is distrust about what is being shared. Making a decision with someone you don't trust requires a lot of extra effort, such as monitoring and enforcing all the rules of process. And where there is trust, there is predictability, a huge contributor to efficiency.

SOMETIMES JUST A CRACK OF QUIET SPACE IS ENOUGH FOR SOME TRUTH TO SNEAK INTO MY THINKING.

I don't think it can be overstated how much trust contributes to efficiency. When I truly trust my decision-making colleagues, I am able to take my eyes off them and let them do their jobs; I can let go of the need for written rules, policies, monitoring, and enforcement. When I can make an agreement based on a handshake or a nod, rather than based on a document, that's efficiency.

When Trust Is Broken

A decision-making group might have a good infrastructure in place and execute the mechanics perfectly, but if the individual members of the group don't trust each other, good results are doomed.

This was the case at a nonprofit organization that I was hired to help with strategic planning. They were a fairly well-established nonprofit, in business for fifty years, and they ran an education center with paid staff. I met with the board chair, the executive director, and senior staff and asked about their situation and why they wanted a strategic plan. The staff especially seemed resistant to strategic planning. There was a passing reference to a previous strategic planning effort, but it was obvious that no one wanted to say too much about it.

Once the planning process got underway, we did a survey of employees, key donors, and stakeholders. Employees were to provide comments anonymously, and the comments would come to me only. This is pretty typical so people feel free to speak their truths.

In those comments I could see a lot of mistrust. In the previous strategic planning effort, things were promised but never delivered. As we discussed in this chapter, the fastest way to erode trust is to say you're going to do something and then not do it. There was a track record of what appeared to be managers saying whatever they thought employees wanted to hear, whatever would keep them quiet in the moment, but then not delivering on expectations. Another very fast way to erode trust is to plant an expectation and not deliver.

This explained perfectly why the employees didn't want to participate in strategic planning. I was a bad guy as far as they

continued

could tell, a puppet of management and a waste of time because no matter how well we might plan, the staff did not trust their managers to follow up one bit.

In fact, they were downright uncooperative with me and didn't want to participate in strategic planning. Understandably. When trust erodes, people drift away, disengage, and detach. In this case the discontent had spread to the volunteers and even among the public whom the organization was serving. An unhelpful culture of management versus staff had developed. To solve this problem, management would need to start building back trust (doing what they say) and staff would need to be open to management's improvements—clumsy as they might be—and praise them when they moved in the right direction.

BE TRANSPARENT

Where open-mindedness is an attitude of accepting all information, transparency is an attitude of being willing to give all information. Having an attitude of transparency means you share things from *within you.* You are willing to share what you know and how you feel. You don't hide or withhold knowledge or information for your own advantage. An attitude of being ready to share information with others is extremely helpful for good group decisions.

Of course, there are times for discretion and not all information should be shared publicly, but when you feel like withholding something, consider your motive. Am I withholding information because I think it's best for the group or best for me? You know where this is headed: It may be OK to withhold information but only when withholding would be best for the group. It's not OK to withhold information for personal gain. Information is power. As a rule, unless otherwise decided on a case-by-case basis, providing information helps others and withholding it hurts others.

Creativity and innovation happen when we all put everything on the table. When people freely share their information and ideas in a collaborative process without regard for credit or blame, they can build something together that no one person could have built on their own. When we all freely share our knowledge and ideas, we all have access to the best available knowledge and ideas and as a group can achieve great things.

Another form of transparency has to do with sharing feelings, different from sharing knowledge. To be transparent with your feelings can make you vulnerable to judgment and critique, even attack. For most people, sharing feelings is way harder than sharing information. Yet sharing feelings is positively essential for good group decisions. Sharing feelings is the first cousin of being authentic. When people don't share feelings as decisions are being made, there will likely be hurt feelings later, when the decision is implemented.

Yet sharing feelings is hard for most of us, downright awkward for many, and "not gonna happen" for some. There is a lot at stake with honesty. Speaking honestly is often not knowing what will come of your words. Speaking honestly might upset the peace. Saying what will please the listener is often way easier. On the other hand, to say what we really feel can bring liberation. Sharing feelings can mean a breakthrough of understanding for a large group of people or a breakthrough deep within ourselves. Telling the truth helps the fear go away and sets us free.

Sometimes just putting your views or feelings on the table

and taking no further steps is enough. For example, two people with a disagreement might simply take turns sharing; each person says what the issue looks like from their perspective and neither one comments on the words of the other. That's all. The disagreement might not become instantly resolved due to this sharing, but then again, it might. And there is additional value in the saying and the hearing. Hearing each other talk brings new perspectives and new understanding no matter if that particular issue gets resolved or not.

"Show up. Pay attention. Speak your truth. And let go of the outcome." A friend, Mary Thayer, used to say that.

"The outcome" of saying your words might look really bad. There might be tears or slamming doors or broken hearts. Or what happens next might look really good. There might be smiles or relief or some sort of leap-ahead breakthrough. But actually—to Mary's point—what happens next after I say my words is not my responsibility. My job is to speak my truth and whatever happens next is not entirely because of my words. I'm never that powerful.

Detaching from the outcome gives me courage to speak my truth. When we understand that we're not responsible for the outcome, only responsible for speaking our truth, it's easier to say what's on our minds. And in our hearts.

Caroline Estes believes that if a group is about to make a decision that in your heart you think is bad for the group, you have a moral obligation to speak up. It doesn't matter whether you want to or not. It doesn't matter if speaking up would be hard for you personally. It's not about you. To ensure your group can make good decisions, your job is to share what you see and feel. No matter what it is.

BE HUMBLE

Just like it's not helpful to think too little of yourself, it's not helpful to think too much of yourself. The best group decisions makers are those who see themselves as a contributing *part* of the group. If I lack humility, I am inclined not to care so much about what other people know or feel. And if I discount what other people know or feel, as a practical matter, I am depriving myself of huge amounts of valuable information.

If I lack humility, I probably think that I know best about what the group should do or how it should conduct its business. If I lack humility, I'm probably not even aware that I am not aware of the best way forward. People without humility want to maintain their appearance of being better than others and pretend to know more than they do. They might bluff or give knowingly false answers, which sets the group up for making decisions based on false (and potentially dangerous) information. A person without humility has blinders on and is often entirely unaware that people think they are doing a bad job. When such a person comes across their own mistakes or oversights, they don't even consider that they themselves might be to blame. A person without humility will rarely answer a question with, "I don't know." And they don't easily admit mistakes.

When we are able to admit that we don't know the answer or don't know what course of action we should take, it encourages us to slow down, gather better information, be patient, and perhaps do nothing. And if it turns out that we don't decide anything because we don't have enough accurate information, that's often fine. At least we don't risk making a bad decision with bad consequences. Doing nothing is vastly underrated in American society.

Another aspect of a humble attitude is asking for help. This can have two very positive results: First, you get help! More resources are brought to bear on the problem and chances are increased that the problem gets solved. Second is that other people get asked a question that leads to their feeling useful. Now it's a group effort instead of an individual effort; you have invited collaborators. Having many people working on shared problems builds group unity and a sense of worth among the participants.

Admitting mistakes is also part of humility and transparency. All humans make mistakes. Sometimes they result from misunderstanding, or from trying to achieve something new, or because of poor judgment. But whatever the cause, the first step if you want to fix it is to see the mistake and say it out loud. If it's your mistake, say it first. Call yourself out. Acknowledging mistakes makes the group better and stronger, and it's critical for individual learning. Learning from small mistakes prevents bigger mistakes. It's never right to judge a person just because they made a mistake. The better basis for judgment is how that person handles the mistake.

I like the story of the business person who made a major mistake. They were the leader of a large division in a large company and they made a mistake costing the company millions of dollars. They talked to the company's president about the mistake. They offered their resignation. They expected to be fired. "Why would I fire you?" the president said. "You are aware of your mistake, right? You have suffered great humiliation, right? You have learned your lesson, right?" The business person answered yes to all these questions. "Then you," the president went on, "are more valuable to me now than ever. And more valuable than anyone I might replace you with, because you are least likely to make such a mistake ever again."

Mistakes are often painful in the short term but useful in the long term. They teach us how to do things better. Admit your mistake, apologize, try to fix it, take stock of lessons learned, and move on. Turn mistakes into opportunities to demonstrate your good character. Graduate from small mistakes to higher stakes.

Finally, no one person, no matter how terrific or influential they are, is ever solely responsible for the successes or failures of a group. No one is that important. Every single person in a decision-making group influences group outcomes, and a lot of things outside the group influence its outcomes too. Show up, pay attention, speak your truth, and let go of the outcome.

CHAPTER 8

For the Good of the Group

WHEN I HAVE an attitude of wanting to help my group—when I believe in community first, when I believe in *we* over *me*—it's natural for me to want to support group processes. I want to learn and honor group customs and group rules. I want to participate in those customs and obey those rules. Actually, I've come to revere such customs and rules. As an American, I love our custom of voting on the first Tuesday of every November. And I support our rule that every single American gets a vote. I uphold and honor our laws about free speech and states' rights. And I honor court decisions.

I understand that rules are in place to help the group as a whole, so I am willing to make personal sacrifices and follow rules for the good of the group. For instance, I don't drive as fast as I might like for the safety of everyone else. I pay taxes so that the money can fund our national defense, education, and roads. I don't litter in public places so those places can be nice for others.

It's the same with smaller groups such as companies and families. For the good of the family, I follow the rule about leaving no dirty dishes in the sink. For the good of my company, I follow the rule about not parking in spaces reserved for visitors.

PUSH REVERENCE

I believe groups make better decisions when they operate with a sense of reverence; that is, when they are serious and focused, when group members feel that something special is happening, when there is extra respect for the moment, for each other, and for something larger than themselves. Reverence is associated with a sense of humility, a sense that more happening in that moment than one person alone can comprehend or control. Indeed, that's exactly the thing about group decisions: it's about more than just me.

Some groups instill reverence by beginning meetings with a pledge or a prayer or at least a call to order. Other groups instill reverence by meeting in a special place or wearing deliberate clothes or using formal speech or titles. Some groups instill reverence by honoring special people from the past. To remember is to bring back a member from the past into the present and imagine their wisdom among us. Other signs of reverence are listening without interruption and turning away from cell phones and other distractions.

Reverence is an outward showing of inward feelings of respect. To be reverent is to signal others that one is doing something special, that one is humble—all qualities that help improve the chances of making good group decisions. You might make group decisions without any sense of reverence, but then how does anyone know to take the decision seriously?

As a practical matter, supporting group rules and customs can help lead to good group decisions by providing predictability, stability, and safety. When people voluntarily follow group rules and customs, it minimizes the need for monitoring and enforcement. As a group we don't have to spend time or money on pushing people to do the right things when they are doing them anyway. Instill reverence into your group decision-making. Be fully present. Show respect for your group process and for each other. These things have practical benefits, not the least of which is increased group efficiency.

KNOW WHEN IT'S TIME TO CHANGE POLICIES

What happens if someone disagrees with a rule or a custom? For example, perhaps my company has a policy of no jeans at work but I like to wear jeans at work. No customers ever see me because I'm in the back of the shop, and they wouldn't care if they did see me wearing jeans anyway, so I think it's a dumb policy. It limits my ability to express myself with my clothes, and it prevents me from being physically comfortable.

Or what about a deeper issue, a rule or policy that I have a moral disagreement with? Perhaps my company has a policy that if a woman becomes pregnant, she gets three months of paid maternity leave but if a man's wife becomes pregnant, he gets just two weeks of paid paternity leave. "That's morally unfair!" I might think. Our society holds both parents legally responsible for raising a child so why shouldn't both parents get equal support for doing so regardless of their gender or where the kid came from? Further, we also know that full attention from both parents supports the strong start of a new life. To support one parent in child-rearing more than the other is bad for families, bad for society, and morally wrong.

Here's how to confront a group policy you disagree with. The first step is to work within the system. All groups—from nations to companies to families—have processes for changing policies, rules, and customs. Regardless of whether the processes are open or closed, all policies, rules, and even customs need to adapt over time to new technologies, new demographics, and new situations. It's called evolution. Groups that are unwilling or unable to change go extinct.

You've got a problem with your company's policy? Step one is raise the issue. Put a note in the suggestion box. Send an email to the human resources director. Take it up with your supervisor. Talk with colleagues about it. Try to craft a solution collaboratively with others. Do the things you're supposed to do within the system. You've got a problem with a state law? Step one is to go to the statehouse and argue for a change. Campaign and vote for state leaders who will change the law. Run for office yourself; be a lawmaker and work to make change from the inside.

Keep in mind that when you try to make change in your company or state or any other group, you will be more successful if you can argue that the change is best for the group (whatever entity it is), not just best for you. If you can't wear jeans to work, it might be bad for you, but is it bad for the company? If both moms and dads can't take a long parental leave, it might be bad for you and it might be bad for society, but is it bad for the company? You have to be able to argue that a change in group policy will *help* that actual group, not just help you personally or help some larger or different group.

If I'm a man whose wife is pregnant, it's not going to work well to go to my boss and argue for longer maternity leave because I want more time at home. Or because it will be good for me and my wife. Or even the kid. I'll have more success if I can make the case that longer maternity leave for both parents will help the *company*—that it will result in happier, more productive employees and help the company recruit more effective employees. Present the evidence and make the case that what you seek is best for the group.

Often, step one doesn't work. A note in the company suggestion box goes nowhere, and a letter to your senator changes nothing—even if you make a "good for the group" case. If you work within the system for change and the change you want does not happen, you have three choices:

1. Leave the group.

2. Accept and conform.

3. Break the rules.[23]

If you have a *we over me* attitude, you could justify breaking a rule if you think that the rule is bad (potentially fatal) for the group as a whole. Another justification could be that you have no other choice. For example, you're trying to get by and feed your family. People steal and cheat and break public laws all the time in order to feed themselves or stay alive, and who am I to say that's not OK? Yet I can say without reservation that it's not OK to break your group rules or a public law for your own

---

23 I'm not talking about just public laws, this applies to breaking the laws or rules of whatever group you are in.

trivial gain. It's not OK to obey the laws you like and disobey the ones you don't like. Such behavior results in the group as a whole—society as a whole in the case of public laws—having to pay the costs of your avoided taxes or litter cleanup or crimes against neighbors. The group also has to pay the increased costs associated with monitoring, enforcement, and punishment for people who don't follow the rules. These costs can be huge for the group.

Civil disobedience—intentionally breaking a rule or law to make a point—has a rightful place in group decision-making but only when the stakes are very high. It's serious stuff. It can result in getting arrested or losing a job, or worse. Yet intentional disobedience can be highly effective when other methods are not. Some even argue that if we have a true *we over me* attitude, we have a moral obligation to break rules or laws that we think are bad for the group over the long run.

The notion that we always have choices—to leave, accept, or break the rules—is a very nice notion, but it only works for privileged people. As a white wealthy male, I often have such choices. Yet many people are not in a position to either leave a group or break a rule. The person in poverty who depends on their job can't actually "leave the group." Many people put up with rules and customs at work, some of them deeply troubling, because they don't dare quit. Very few of us are in a position to break a rule—to take a stand or make a point—because it could get us shunned or fired or banished or beat up or killed. And many people don't even dare suggest a change—by anonymous suggestion box or not—for fear of retribution.

People in oppressive relationships have no choice but to accept and live with a hard situation. When it's not a choice, it's called oppression. In the United States, oppression happens more to people of color, to poorer people, to women, and to people with nonconforming genders or sexual preferences. Those of us who are not so oppressed can help by speaking up and acting on behalf of those who don't have such privilege. When I am in a leadership position, I make extra efforts to give everyone a say, especially those who are often shut out or shut down. And when I see oppressive behavior limiting the potential of my group, I try to call it out and maybe take action.

Honoring group rules and customs (and making sure they are applied evenly to all) is an easy way to demonstrate to others that you are a *we first* person rather than a *me first* person. Especially if you are in a leadership position, when you follow group rules and customs, you're telling everyone it's cool to follow group rules and customs. That builds support among others for following group rules and customs. And you know what? It contributes greatly to the group efficiency when the group doesn't have to spend a lot of time arguing about or enforcing group rules and customs. Groups can get so much more done when enforcing rules is not a distraction.

KNOW THE RULES. BUILD RELATIONSHIPS. DO BOTH.

Some people put a lot of stock in relationships and build trust that people will do the right thing. Two business partners take a risk together, perhaps even outside the rules or off the map, but they do it because of faith in their relationship. "I don't know how it will turn out but if they are my partner it will be OK," they each say to themselves.

Some people put a lot of stock in rules (defined broadly to include roles, cultural norms, and processes) and build trust that a framework of rules and customs where everyone knows and plays their roles. Two coworkers dislike each other, but the company's established rules, roles, and boundaries allow them to work effectively together. There's trust in the institutional infrastructure to keep them both safe.

Most groups are tangled webs of rules and relationships. As in the examples above, when rules don't work, relationships take over. When relationships don't work, rules take over. To accommodate all personality types, it's good for a group to have both: good rules and good relationships. Whenever your group has a problem, consider whether the fix should involve building relationships and/or making or enforcing rules. And be sure to question your own behavior. "Am I investing in the relationship? Am I following the rules? Do I need to propose a new rule?" Basically: "Here's what I see happening. Here's the array of possible responses. What am I going to do to help fix this?" Here's an example from a school board I worked with, told from the perspective of one of the board members.

Mabel on the School Board

I'd been on a school board for two or three years and I'd come to know a fellow member, Mabel. She'd been on the school board for twenty-three years and had some old-fashioned and unhelpful ideas about the role that school board members should play. A parent had recently come to her (this parent was also a neighbor of hers and knew Mabel outside of school) and complained about how their child was being treated by a teacher. Mabel jumped in and said, "OK, I'm going to help you with this problem" and arranged a meeting between the parent and the teacher and Mabel to talk through the situation.

Mabel thought she should act as the parent's advocate and that her role was to help parents get their needs met. But this was not the school board policy. The policy stated that when a member of the school board is approached by a parent or member of the community with a complaint, that complaint should get passed on to the principal of the particular school. Mabel's first question to the parent/neighbor should have been: "Have you talked to your teacher or principal about this directly?" As a fellow school board member, I thought Mabel's actions were a problem. A teacher needs to have one boss, and that is their principal or supervisor.

So, what was the best way to approach this problem? Work on rules or work on relationships? If I thought the problem could be fixed with relationship building, maybe I could have coffee with Mabel, get to know her a little bit, and get inside her head—or, frankly, let her inside mine. I could allow myself to be vulnerable and that would open doors to conversations with her about personal things and why she behaved as she did. And maybe it would open up space for me to tell her why I thought her behavior was not OK.

If I thought it was a rule problem, then Mabel would need to be called out. If she was repeatedly intervening between parents and teachers, that would not be OK and someone would need to say something about it and maybe do something about it. The group would simply need to enforce its rules and even punish Mabel or kick her off the board if needed.

Chances are this problem wouldn't need to be fixed by *making* new rules. It would be worth considering, but a rule already says that Mabel shouldn't have done what she did. If there's already a good rule, don't make a new one. Groups often make new policies because that's easier than enforcing old ones, but continually making new rules to fix what's really an enforcement issue is inefficient and imposes future inefficiencies on the group.

I could see different possible responses to Mabel's actions. But I couldn't let my first reaction determine my final decision. I needed to consider all of the options before acting.

I also needed to consider my own behavior. I could sit on the other side of the table from Mabel all day long and think thoughts like "Yeah, somebody needs to do something about that" or "Yeah, Mabel needs to resign" or "Yeah, the teachers should not agree to have meetings with Mabel." I could think thoughts like that, or I could think "What am I going to do about this?"

I needed to fully consider my own responsibility in this challenge faced by the group as a whole. How had I enabled Mabel? Her behavior happened within a system; what about the system enabled and empowered her to do this? I probably found I had some guilt there. Mabel had done this sort of thing several times before and I hadn't spoken up. Nor had I ever had coffee with her and gotten to know her.

As a good fellow board member to Mabel, I made sure not only to consider all the approaches to changing Mabel's behavior, but also how I was going to change my behavior to help fix the problem.

VALUE ALL GIFTS

I will never meet a single person who cannot do at least one thing better than me. Most people can do many, many things better than me. Rather than be intimidated or threatened by the ability of others or make them my enemy, I welcome their gifts.

When I look for someone's gifts, there are two practical advantages. First, I might find that the person has relevant gifts (talents, contacts, resources) that I can match with the group's needs. Second, by seeking the best in another person, I build my rapport and credibility with the person. It's going to make it easier to work with this person on the issues where we disagree, because I have treated them kindly and positively and with encouragement rather than discouragement.

I WILL NEVER MEET A SINGLE PERSON WHO CANNOT DO AT LEAST ONE THING BETTER THAN ME.

To do all we can to improve the chances of good group decisions, we foster giving. And that means always looking for gifts and gratefully receiving them. We encourage participation, inclusiveness, and creativity. We don't view new people to the group as threatening; instead, we trust they will give to the group rather than take away from it.

In meetings, because we are always seeking gifts, we try to hear every perspective. When we believe that there is good in everyone, we believe that every person has something good to offer the conversation. Each person has a gift to give. We make space for all to contribute.

This practice also highlights the importance of silence in a group. Silence is like standing by an open door and gesturing for someone else to go first. It is holding back to hear what others have to say. Silence is waiting for the next gift.

INSIGHT: Figure Out Who Has the Hot Hand

Some people are better at some things than others, and we all have our good days and bad days. I know of a basketball coach who encourages his team to shoot around before every game and figure out who has the "hot hand"—who seems to be particularly gifted that day. Get the ball into the hands of that person, he encourages.

For any given task on any given day, figure out who is most suited to lead. Who has the gift that day. It could be anyone. If you are not the most able person, for whatever reason, support someone who is. Members of high-functioning groups are flexible and give the ball to the person who is most likely to succeed in the moment, regardless of prior established titles, positions, or plans.

PART III

PRACTICES

CHAPTER 9

Creating a Vision, Mission, and Goals

WHEN IT COMES to making good group decisions, members of the group have to want similar things for the future. But how can groups define those wants and put them into practice? Well, it starts with a strong foundation. Every group needs common ground to build from so they can not only survive but thrive. Many groups refer to their foundation as their vision, mission, and goals.

SHAPING YOUR VISION FOR THE FUTURE

While storytellers help us see what we *have* in common, leaders help us see what we *want* in common. Leaders gather groups around ideas of how things can be better. Leaders articulate *visions*.

Saying how the future could be better for a given group attracts people to the group. For instance, the Nature Conservancy holds a vision for a world where "the diversity of life thrives." If you hold that vision, you are probably drawn to join the organization or support its work. The American Red Cross holds a vision for a society in which "all people affected by disaster . . . receive care, shelter, and hope." If you hold that vision, you are probably drawn to join that organization or support its work.

People are drawn to general ideas that make them feel better about the future or themselves. Shared visions are "put out there," and people select for the extent of their participation in, or commitment to, all the visions out there. When a vision is articulated (written or spoken or streamed), people gather or not—naturally. Complete or detailed visions don't have to be perfect at the start. Indeed, they never are. Visions are often initiated and promoted by leaders, but the best visions are developed over time in groups, building on previous ideas and refining the shared vision.

People join causes not committees. People get excited about products not processes. For a group of people to be enthusiastic about participating, they need to be enthusiastic about the possibilities. A vision—a promise of a better future—is the highest motivator of human beings. When we are motivated by fear or threat, we are inclined to do only as much as needed. When the fear or threat is gone completely, so is our motivation. When we are compelled by fear or threat, we are looking behind us and we are driven by negativity. But when we are compelled by the promise of a brighter future, we are looking forward and we have infinite energy to achieve our dreams. Highly effective groups attract people because of the good things that might happen if they join, rather than because of the bad things that might happen if they don't join. If you have been moved by a gospel hymn or an ad for underwear, you have received a message that says: "If you like this vision, join us." Visions for a better future compel participation.

Just so there is no confusion, there are two types of vision statements. Some organizations have what they call a vision statement that describes their future organization, where they are headed as an organization, a vision of themselves in the future. Another type is a statement that describes a future world—how we would like things to be different in the future, how we want to see our community change, how we want things to look out there in the world. A statement that describes how the organization wants itself to be in the future can be extremely useful, but I prefer to call that a "statement of strategic direction" or whatever other term you like, but not to be confused with a vision statement. In my opinion, it's more useful when a vision statement describes a future world, not the future organization. The statement that describes your future organization, call that something else.

WHAT'S YOUR MISSION?

Where a vision statement expresses how we want the world to be better, an organization's mission statement expresses what we are going to do about it. Further, an organization's goals and objectives and other aspects of what might be called a "strategic plan" are additional specific statements about what the organization plans to do. A strategic plan is the mission broken down into pieces.

While many groups may be working to achieve a relatively shared vision—such as world peace or clean water or a growing economy—each group has a different method of working to achieve that vision, and with a different geographic focus. In other words, shared vision but different missions.

In addition to describing what a group does and where it does it, a group's mission and goals define the boundaries of what it doesn't do and where it doesn't do things. It's helpful for an organization to say: "Here's what we do and where we do it. And we do not do anything else."

Of course, this is a simplistic view. In reality the boundaries of what a group does and where it works are complicated. The Mid Coast Hunger Prevention Program is focused on providing healthy food to people in my part of Maine, yet the organization's leaders meet regularly with food pantry leaders from other parts of the state. And they also meet with other leaders that have little to do with providing food, such as the local fire chief, the police chief, and local business owners. While the organization's primary focus is to provide food in a certain way in a certain place, secondary activities stray outside those lines a bit, which is fine so long as those activities have some clear connection to the mission and goals.

INSIGHT: Think About What It Looks Like to Achieve

As a group or as an individual, doors unlock for you if you can determine what you want. Define it. Visualize it. Think about how much fun it's going to be to get there. Groups often steam ahead without nearly enough thought or cohesion about what they are trying to achieve. Groups often don't invest enough in defining their goals. If you don't determine a goal, you can't be accused of failing to achieve it. Honestly, I think this is why some people and some groups resist getting clarity from the start; it's a setup for accountability.

> Winning is not just hard work and persistence: It starts with defining a goal. It really helps to know what the successful end looks like and feels like. Such knowing and determination naturally motivate hard work and persistence.
>
> In 2014, Mikaela Shiffrin won an Olympic gold medal in women's slalom skiing. In interviews she explained that for years she had visualized herself winning that gold medal. She had a vision, and it was so defined that it compelled her to be very focused and work very hard to achieve it. While she was riding the ski lift on the way up for her gold medal run, alone on a double-chair, reporters noticed a silent tear through their telephoto lenses. When asked about it later, she explained that it was a tear of joy. She explained that she could see herself winning the gold medal. She knew she was about to do it. And just before the start of her run at the top of the mountain, one can notice a slight smile to herself in the video. I think that smile meant "This is gonna be fun."

It is important that a group's leader or a specific committee not stray so far outside the mission and goals that members lose sight of their purpose. This can be done by adhering to the organization's strategic plan or strategic direction and by the board of directors receiving reports not just about the organization's activities but how those activities support the goals. Repeat: institutionalize progress reporting that is organized along the lines of the strategic plan.

Often, activities start happening in an organization that don't align with any goals. When that happens, a decision must be made to either change the activities or change the goals. It's pretty simple. The trick is to be deliberate about noticing when a practice is out of line with policy and do something about it. Either change the writing of the goals or change the actions in the field.

INSIGHT: How to Say No

Jim Collins, the author of *Good to Great* and other books, reminds us that great organizations (groups) have "piercing clarity" about what they want to achieve and "relentless discipline" to say no to diversions.[24] Successful groups identify and continually affirm their most important goals by establishing strategic plans and keeping those plans front and center. With every opportunity to say yes or no to a new thing, successful groups ask, "How does this help achieve what's most important?"

Beware: It's way harder to say no than to say yes. As a member of any group, it is almost always easier to quietly agree than to take an opposing stand. Imagine a group planning an annual picnic. When they start making the menu, it's wonderful. All sorts of ideas and things get added. When they match their ideas against their budget, they are confronted with cuts. People don't shout out their ideas for cuts with nearly as much enthusiasm as they shouted ideas for adds.

One trick is to try to keep things off the list in the first place. If it doesn't help a goal, the answer is no. Practice saying something like: "That's a good idea, I understand and appreciate your perspective, but that simply doesn't fit with our priorities right now." Or "That might be good for someone else, or good for us at another time, but it's just not good for us right now." And if you are asking a group to make a list—like the menu for the annual picnic—start by telling them the budget.

---

24 Jim Collins, *Good to Great: Why Some Companies Make the Leap and Others Don't* (HarperBusiness, 2001).

STRATEGIC PLANNING BASICS

Strategic planning means different things to different people. Some people have very specific ways of going about it and how things are defined. Yet I figure that if you have something in writing with the following three qualities, you can call it a strategic plan.

First, it needs to be long-term. A strategic plan is more than just the annual work plan or the annual budget. It's usually set up for two years, five years, ten years, or longer.

Second, it's comprehensive. It covers all the different aspects of the organization. Not just the programs that you're going to run but also the administrative and institutional stuff like board development if you have a board and staff development if you have staff. It also includes the financial plans for capital improvements. If you're a nonprofit, it includes the plans for fundraising, where you're going to get the money, and how you're going to spend the money. How detailed you want to get is a matter of choice—goals, objectives, strategies, performance metrics, etc.—but I think to be truly strategic, the plan needs to say at least a little bit about everything that the organization (or division of an organization) does.

Third, the organization's leadership must be involved. Someone two levels down can't make a plan for the whole organization and call it a strategic plan. A true strategic plan needs to be embraced by whoever is in charge of making it happen, the people who are actually implementing long-term strategy for the organization.

Strategic planning is an opportunity for an organization or group to rise above the day-to-day operations and look further to the future. It's a chance to take stock of big trends affecting the organization. It's a chance to evaluate the organization's strengths, weaknesses, and opportunities—and plan accordingly.

Elements of a Simple Strategic Plan

Vision: How we want things to be different or better in our world (whatever "world" it is that our group is concerned with).

Mission: What our organization is going to do in order to achieve the vision, especially the things we are uniquely suited to do.

Situation: A basic description of our organization including some version of our strengths, weaknesses, opportunities, and threats (known as a SWOT analysis). Might include a competition analysis, market analysis, and/or stakeholder input.

Goals: Multiple goals for the organization. One for each major area of work. Each goal is a carefully worded statement of what we expect to accomplish in each area.

Objectives: Multiple objectives for each goal. Statements about smaller pieces of what we expect to accomplish. Objectives often contain a statement that makes them measurable, such as an expectation to achieve _____ (a number that can be monitored) by _____ (a date).

Strategies: Multiple strategies for each objective. Some strategies might serve multiple objectives. Strategies are write-ups of your plans for achieving your objectives—how you're going to do it and including what people and resources you will need.

It works well to have two types of goals: what and how. _What goals_ are what the public sees—or what the organization does. This part of the plan is about programs and activities. _How goals_ are behind the scenes, or how the stuff gets done. That part of the plan covers staffing, facilities, governance, finances, etc. One of the strategies should describe how the organization is going to monitor progress and revise the strategic plan. Build it in.

Many organizations invest in strategic planning every few years since the idea is to not wait for a crisis that suddenly needs to be handled. Even absent an apparent crisis or big decision to be made, take stock of the situation and surroundings in your organization or group so you can better anticipate the next big decision and prevent the next big crisis.

Strategic plans in whatever form they may take are useful for many reasons. Groups use their strategic plan to attract employees, investors, and donors. The plan gives potential partners of all types a good picture of where their organization is headed. Groups use the strategic plan as a way to hold key officers/ employees responsible and accountable. It's an excellent tool for both accountability and for celebrating progress. Groups use the strategic planning process to work through and make hard decisions. Also the process can be super useful for gathering input from stakeholders and taking a good look at the environment in which the group exists. For many groups, actually, the process itself is what is most valuable.

Whatever your reason for strategic planning, it's important to spend the right amount of effort; that is, the effort must be in proportion to the amount of benefit you're going to get from it. Strategic planning has gotten a bad reputation in the world because so often these efforts are not right-sized. The biggest complaint is that strategic planning is too involved and requires too much effort in proportion to any good that might come from it. Another complaint is that the resulting plan is too vague or based on too many assumptions, to the point of being useless. To maximize reward for your participants, know at the outset why you want a strategic plan and don't push people through a process that's too complicated or too simple to get what you need.

How do you keep your strategic plan alive? Here are three ideas:

1. Organize your plan like your work.

Let's say your strategic plan has four goals. Think about having four committees, one assigned to each goal. Or if you have four managers, have them manage operations in alignment with the four goals. Or rather than trying to fit your work to match your plan, fit your plan to match your work. If your company does four basic types of things, organize your plan along those four lines of business. This might seem oversimplistic or even impractical, but as much as you can organize your plan to be aligned with how you actually do your work, it will help keep your plan alive.

2. Report regularly on the progress.

Many boards of directors or corporate management teams have regular meetings where participants state, "Here's what we did since we last met." But rarely do those reports align with the strategic plan. Whoever's running the meeting should insist that every report not just be a random "Here's what we did" but "Here's what we did to support the strategic plan." Do not spend time making or listening to reports that don't have a place in the plan.

3. Change the map or the course.

If your team drifts from the plan, don't pretend you don't see it or hope it will be OK. Call it out. Simply notice out loud that what you're doing is different from what you had planned. Then do one of two things—either put a stop to the drift or change the plan to match the drift. And let me tell you, it's totally fine to change the plan. That's actually how you keep it alive—by making it adaptable and changeable and in continuous alignment with your actual practices.

CHAPTER 10

Degrees of Membership

WHEN A GROUP wants to make good decisions that accomplish its goals, it's important to get the right people on board. This is why clarity about vision, mission, and goals—and being able to communicate those to others—is so important. It helps someone decide whether they should be a member of the group, and it helps leaders decide who should be involved and in what way.

If your group lacks a clear vision, it's going to attract people with different visions. Assembling such a team often results in either conflict between the team members or an end product that is a useless hodgepodge of individual ideas and expertise. On the other hand, when you gather a team around a clear vision and you're deliberate about making sure that each team member understands and believes in the vision, there is a much less chance of conflict among team members and a much greater chance of a magnificent end product.

Having a clear mission, vision, and goals to attract the right people doesn't just apply to established groups with written charters. It also applies to temporary groups that we are all a part of—meetings. Every meeting where people intend to make a decision should have some sort of stated purpose. It could be a formal sentence or two written on an agenda, but it can also be an informal one like, "Hey, the reason I called you guys together is to work through the Johnson account and make a decision about who's going to do what next to get this thing wrapped up by next week." This helps people decide if they should attend and it provides guidance about how the meeting should be structured. Meetings without clear goals that are understood by the participants are almost always a waste of time. Meetings with clear goals have a much better chance of garnering the participation of the right people and, therefore, a much better chance of getting decisions made and things done.

If you make big and wide goals for your group, you can gather a lot of people. If your goals touch hearts, you can gain enthusiasm and loyalty. Great leaders establish or affirm visions and goals that people really want to give their time and effort to—making it more than just a job.

There's the story of the four bricklayers on a construction site: When asked what they were doing, the first said, "Laying a brick"; the second said, "Building a wall"; the third said, "Building a cathedral"; and the fourth said, "Serving God." They each saw themselves connected to the project differently. Which bricklayer do you think put the most into their work? Which bricklayer do you think liked their job the most?

INSIGHT: What's the Right Size Group?

If you want each person to have a sense of ownership in the group, the ideal size is three to five people. When too many people are involved, one or more people will think "someone else will take care of that" and give up ownership.

It's interesting that many immediate families—at least around me—number two to five people. In our culture, most of us are accustomed to making decisions with others in a family structure. Perhaps this suggests that groups resembling families, loosely defined, are likely to work well.

Want a group to discuss and come to agreement as a group? Three to five is a great number for that too. And it's common to find in business literature that no one should supervise more than five people. If someone has to supervise more than five, the quality of many aspects of good supervision (communication, mentoring, accountability, etc.) suffers greatly.

WHAT'S YOUR STAKE?

Even in the most inclusive and democratic groups, not all members are equal, ever. For one thing it depends on your stake—where you sit relative to the action. How involved you get in every decision depends on how much you care about it. How much do you have to lose? Or to win? It also depends on how much relative power you have, or privilege. Every group and every issue attract people in varying degrees. Some people are really into it. Some are on the fringes. And that's totally fine and as it should be. But it's helpful when the degrees of participation are clearly defined and everyone knows where they stand. That's the trick.

6. DEGREES OF MEMBERSHIP

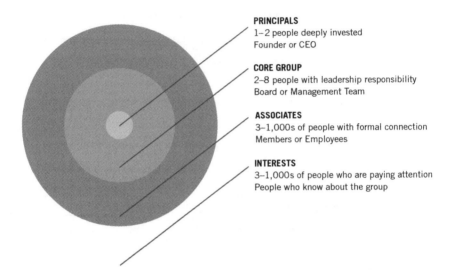

PRINCIPALS
1–2 people deeply invested
Founder or CEO

CORE GROUP
2–8 people with leadership responsibility
Board or Management Team

ASSOCIATES
3–1,000s of people with formal connection
Members or Employees

INTERESTS
3–1,000s of people who are paying attention
People who know about the group

The diagram of the degrees of membership illustrates the four degrees of membership, simply named touchstones among the vast array of how people participate in groups. All people, no matter which degree of membership they fall into, have a stake in what the group does. Even those with a passing interest are members of the wider community touched by the group's activities.

This diagram could apply to a free-standing organization or to a division or to a sub-group nested within a larger group. It can also apply to a specific project or short-term group. And as an individual, you will be a different type of member in each of the groups you participate in and at different times. Let's take a look at each of the five degrees of group membership:

PRINCIPALS

In a company, the principals are the one or two people who own all or most of the shares. In a family, these are the parents. In a city government, this is the mayor or the city manager. If a group or project is nested within a larger organization, the principals are the one or two people "on the hook" to their supervisors for the success of the thing.

If we ask an outsider about a group, they are likely to name these one or two people as the leaders or the public persona of the group. These are the ones who go to sleep each night and wake up each day thinking about how to make the group better. These are the ones who actually feel, in their bones, the group's triumphs and sorrows. For the group to make any major changes in direction, these people need to be on board. Stuff doesn't happen without their support.

For a group to stay alive there needs to be at least one person whose personal achievements are bound together with the group's achievements and who is willing to stake their reputation on the group's success—who takes some ownership.

CORE GROUP

In a for-profit or nonprofit organization, the core group is the board of directors. In a city government, this is the city council. In a management setting, this is the leadership team, senior management team, or executive group. This is the group of people responsible for running the place. As a whole, the group has the wisdom, workers, and wealth to get the job done. People with "wisdom" have expertise and give advice. People who "work" do volunteer jobs. People with "wealth" give money and serve as conduits to funding. Each member of the core group should care about the group's mission to the point of willingness to make sacrifices for the group. These people want to give to the group because they believe in it. When the group does well, they feel it in their hearts. And when the group does poorly, they feel that too.

In addition, ideally, the core group has representatives of people impacted by the mission of the organization. The principals are often part of this group and have extra influence in this group. Such groups nested within larger organizations are often called committees, work groups, and action teams.

ASSOCIATES

This category includes anyone with any kind of formal membership status. In a company, these are the employees. In a nonprofit, these are the members who pay dues. In a town, these are the residents. In a country, these are the citizens.

INTERESTS

Here we are talking about "the wider community," people who know about the group's activities and follow from a distance. The level of interest varies greatly from person to person and from time to time. Someone with an interest might become more or less involved over time depending on what the group is working on. If a group is a country for instance, other countries have an interest.

ISSUE STAKEHOLDERS

These are the people whose interest gets heightened due to a specific issue that the group is dealing with. In city government, these are the people lobbying at city hall. In *The Office*, this is the party planning committee.[25] In a family, this is the teenager who suddenly becomes interested in the family decision about the next car to be bought. Depending on the issue, some stakeholders may get very involved with the core group or principals while trying to resolve an issue. Certain people can become temporary insiders on certain issues.

WHAT'S YOUR PLACE?

In the previous section, I implied that one can move freely about the degrees of membership based on one's preferences. I implied that with each organization or issue that a person comes across, they get to decide their level of involvement. And this is often true for me. I'm a white man of means in a place where white men of means are privileged. But many people are locked out of many types of membership because of how they look and thus are unable to participate in group decisions that matter to them. They don't have a place in the room where it happens.[26]

It's not useful to pretend that we're all created equal. Unlike me, many people were created non-white, created female, or created in poverty.[27] And these things matter. What you look like and

---

25 Popular situation comedy in which the Party Planning Committee was activated and disbanded depending on, well, the situation.

26 Yes, that's a *Hamilton* reference.

27 I am highlighting discrimination based on race, sex, and wealth because these are the three that I see most often and these are the three around which, historically, there seems to be the most violence in the world. Some say there are five primary dimensions of prejudice: age, gender, sexual orientation, ethnicity, and race. Everything I say applies to *all* types of discrimination and bias. These three—race, sex, and wealth—are simply my leading examples.

where you come from and how you talk matter. Because when I see or hear you, it instantly unlocks suitcases of assumptions that I have been packing for years. It's called baggage, and most of it is not useful and gets in the way.

PRACTICAL REASONS FOR INCLUSION

Many moral arguments are made for treating all people the same regardless of race, ethnicity, gender, sexual preference, wealth, age, etc. My own Quaker values, for instance, preach that there is that of God in every single person and that I should welcome all people of all types with an open heart. Yet there are also profoundly practical reasons for minimizing discrimination and maximizing inclusion. It absolutely helps your group make good decisions.

For one thing, multiple perspectives on an issue provide a fuller picture. As a decision maker I want to see the fullest picture I can of whatever I'm deciding about. This means hearing from those who will be affected by the decision, or at least their representatives, if need be. Even if I make a decision that ends up hurting some of these people, shouldn't I go in with my eyes open? With a full understanding of the situation and the potential consequences? To make a decision with blinders on or with your fingers in your ears seems morally wrong. Yet it's also a tactical mistake to make group decisions without at least considering all the key perspectives that exist among your group.

THERE ARE ALSO PROFOUNDLY PRACTICAL REASONS FOR MINIMIZING DISCRIMINATION.

It's hard work to listen closely to and understand people different from you. For starters, you have to make an effort to get them in the room or meet them where they're at. Differing accents are a distraction, even a barrier. Different customs and ways of speaking need to be accommodated. Frankly, it's easiest to not accommodate such inconveniences at all, especially if you think you already know what's best for the group. Yet benefits accrue when you can accept that you actually don't know best and you are willing to let the group be creative. If you want to do even more and push the group to be creative, work hard to deliberately include otherwise marginalized voices. Creative solutions are hatched when all views and ideas are blended together.

If I'm a group leader and I want the best possible outcomes for the group, I am always working to include key perspectives. I work especially hard to lift voices not normally heard. I actually don't treat all people equal. I give extra encouragement and supports to those who would otherwise be less engaged, and I put protocols in place to contain the louder and traditionally dominant voices. Such protocols include agendas, ground rules, and neutral facilitation. Deliberately encouraging marginalized people to participate is different from providing equal opportunity for marginalized people to participate. Here's an example: "Every citizen has equal opportunity to vote at the Lincoln School on Wednesday afternoon from X p.m. to X p.m." Let's imagine that the Lincoln School is a long way from my part of town. If I'm poor, I can't afford the means to get there. If I'm a mom, I can't manage my kids and vote in the middle of the afternoon. What looks like equal opportunity—anyone can walk in and vote—often shuts out whole classes of people. Providing an equal opportunity to participate is not enough if you want real inclusion, real understanding of all the perspectives, and real creativity and innovation.

FROM WHERE I SIT

If you are not white, not male, or not financially secure, I don't know what you should do in the face of racism, sexism, or classism. I don't know your story. I don't know what place you are coming from. My part is to not speak for or say what's right for you. Repeat: it's not for me to say what's right for others.

To use my privilege for good, here are some other things I try to do:

I accept that prejudices are built into our social systems and that I myself contribute to racism, sexism, and classism. These things are systemic. I'm a player in the system. It's disingenuous for me to pretend that I'm not part of the problem.

I accept that my people—white Europeans—committed genocide and slavery, which laid the foundation for the privileges I have today.

I try to call out racism, sexism, classism, or other discrimination when I see it in others—and I try to catch myself when I see it in myself.

I make room for other voices that don't traditionally get heard. And if I don't get a chance to speak at all, that's fine.

I listen to those with lived experiences and let them lead. If I want to learn how to handle alcoholism, I ask alcoholics. If I want to learn the history of the Indigenous peoples of Maine, I read their versions of their story.

I don't expect things from a person just because they're part of a specific group. If someone is a trans person, I don't ask them to explain what trans means and why they are trans. If a person is Asian, I don't expect them to tell me what this or that looks like from an Asian perspective. If I know someone well enough to ask them personal questions, I do my homework first and learn the terms and other things that I can get from books and articles. I make an effort.

I support self-determination. As a show of respect, I ask each person what they want to be called and then I use their chosen pronouns. The whole rainbow of genders and sexual preferences is fine with me. It's a matter of personal freedom. You might call it individual liberty. Live and let live.

If there's a proposed law that hurts women, I don't leave it to the women to do the fighting. To stand by Black people, I show up to be counted on the streets and by contributing money. Even though I don't feel discrimination myself, I can be extremely helpful. I can freely give away my privileged resources, and I can try to be a role model for how to be in right-relationship with those who are different from me. I don't know how to do this well, but I'm learning. And trying.

Three Elephants: Three Parables of Inclusion and Prejudice

1) There's the story of the **blind men describing an elephant**. The one holding the tail says an elephant is like a rope. The one holding a leg says an elephant is like a tree trunk. The one holding an ear says an elephant is like a cloth. The one holding the trunk says an elephant is like a hose. Only by including and listening to all the perspectives can they put the pieces together and understand what an elephant is really like.

2) Then there's the **elephant and the rider**, who sits on the elephant and tells it where to go. The whole package—elephant and

continued

rider—is your brain. The rider is what your brain has conscious control over. The elephant is the rest of your brain and all those neurological processes that you have no control over. The rider is making decisions to be sure, but the elephant is making decisions too, that the rider doesn't even notice. The elephant is making threat/no-threat decisions with everything it encounters, with every step. The elephant represents your instincts that have accumulated from years of experience and from what people have told you. Your instincts are often misguided and prejudiced. Most of your brain might instinctively recoil at the sight of someone different from you, like the elephant that comes across a zebra and recoils. Most of your brain is instinctively prejudiced. Yet the good news is that you, as the rider, can change the elephant part of your brain to not be afraid of zebras. You can train the elephant (you can train your brain) to get comfortable among zebras. You can actually rewire your instincts, with effort.

3) And, of course, there's **the elephant in the room**—that really big issue that everyone can see but that no one wants to talk about. Often, the "elephant" is a significant power imbalance. We can all see that certain people are getting walked over or will get trampled later, but we pretend we don't see it. When you see an elephant, at least say: "I see an elephant." And say what it looks like from your perspective.[28]

---

28 Jonathan Haidt, *The Righteous Mind: Why Good People Are Divided by Politics and Religion* (New York: Random House, 2012)

CHAPTER 11

Meetings and Facilitation

UNLIKE AN EMAIL, text, post, or paper document, real-time meetings provide a chance for me to say something to you and for you to react instantly and for me to react to you and then for you to react to me. Over and over. Lightning fast. Simultaneously among many people. Meetings are where things get discussed, minds get changed, and group decisions get made. Meetings are special because they provide multiple ways to communicate instantly. Meetings are the fertile ground for leap-ahead understanding and breakthrough creativity. They're kind of a big deal.

In my opinion, a meeting is something that happens in real time and is interactive. There are many ways to conduct real-time interactive meetings: conference call, video, in person, and even group chat if everyone is engaged at the same time and responsive. If people are in the same place at the same time and spontaneously interact somehow, you can call it a meeting.

I like to look at the start of a meeting like the start of an adventure, like the start of a hot air balloon ride. We have prepared the balloon and studied about ballooning. We are up on the weather and have checked the equipment. We are dressed warmly. The balloon holds us in our basket two feet off the ground, tethered. We are secure. We have everything we need on board. As the meeting begins, we let go of the tethers. Anything could happen. We could end up anywhere. It's good to be open to the magic of the moment and not fight it. Where will the wind take us?

WAYS TO MEET

I believe that the chances for productivity increase in proportion to the closeness of the participants. The following diagram shows how much data can be exchanged between people in four basic types of meetings: group chat, video, conference call, and in person. A higher volume of rapid interactive data exchange equates to higher productivity. By data, I'm talking about words, sounds, visual images, smells, observable order of events, and participants' instant reactions—all that stuff you take in when you are in a room with people. As you can see in the diagram, in-person meetings allow for a huge amount of data exchange relative to other methods, which gives them potential to be the most productive.

I'm not saying in-person meetings should always be chosen over other methods. In-person meetings often have the highest costs due to scheduling and travel. I'm saying that to maximize the overall productivity of your employees or your group, you should choose your meeting type carefully. Don't invest in meetings any more than you have to. Yet don't invest too little either. Although in-person meetings are a bigger investment, the payoff can be huge. Meeting magic is more likely to happen the more real-time data is exchanged. If you just want to get messages delivered or get stuff done, don't meet.

7. VOLUME & SPEED OF DATA EXCHANGE BY MEETING TYPE

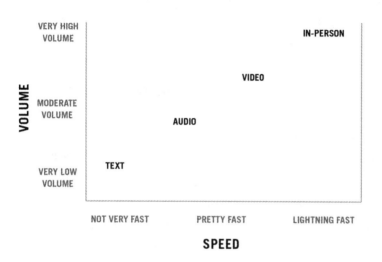

GROUP CHAT – CONFERENCE CALL – VIDEO CALL – IN-PERSON MEETING

In a chat meeting where we exchange written words only, you receive limited data about what the other person or persons are thinking or feeling since you can't see or hear them.

In a conference call you can hear tone of voice and you also learn a lot by how fast or how slow someone reacts, and if or when they interrupt. Just these two things—tone and pace—can tell us a lot! We try to convey tone of voice in writing but it's very hard to do, especially across cultures or with people who don't know us well. Consider the sizes of different types of files on your computer. A Word document takes up so much less space on your computer than an audio file, because audio files contain so much more information.

In a video call you get tone of voice and sense of pace, but you also get some facial expressions and body language. Even though limited to a screen, perhaps a very small screen, seeing whatever you can of a person's face can instantly give you more information. Experts believe that much more is conveyed through facial expressions and body language than can possibly be conveyed with spoken or written words. And you get to see the person in context, what's behind them, the room they are in, and what they are wearing. That's data too.

And, of course, we transmit and absorb the largest amount of data in face-to-face, in-person meeting. Huge amounts. Lightning fast. Not only do you get written and spoken words but you can check out the other participants. And they are checking you out. And you get to see who talks with who. And because you are a human being, you are skilled at assessing group culture just by watching group dynamics. It's very hard to assess group dynamics, mood, or culture through screens or speakers.

Although it differs by type of meeting, all meetings provide fertile ground for collective energy, shared enthusiasm, and that sense of excitement that comes with being part of something bigger than yourself. There is nothing like being in a meeting with a group and knowing that you see things the same way, that you all agree on something, that as a group you share something that each one of you helped create.

AGENDAS ARE PLANS FOR PRODUCTIVITY

Before a meeting can create new benefits for the group, some-one has to create the meeting. For starters, every meeting needs a purpose. Getting clear about why you are meeting and what you hope to achieve is the most important part of planning a meeting. What does the meeting hope to achieve? Can the goal be accomplished in some other way? If you are about to have a meeting and can't state the purpose, don't have the meeting.

Once there is clarity about why a meeting is needed, all other aspects of meeting design should flow from that: the agenda, the participants, the room setup or online platform, the timing, the duration, and so forth. Every meeting should have a purpose and an agenda—even if just an informal "We're meeting today to plan tomorrow's site review and I'd like to make sure we discuss hours, equipment, and roles." (This statement contains the reason for the meeting and a simple list of topics.)

A good agenda sets out the plan for the meeting. It lists what topics will be covered, in what order, and how much time is allowed for each topic. An agenda also states the start and end time of the meeting, where it is to be held, and any other useful information that helps participants know what to expect.

IF YOU ARE ABOUT TO HAVE A MEETING AND CAN'T STATE THE PURPOSE, DON'T HAVE THE MEETING.

An agenda serves as a time management tool that shows the participants at the start, the complete list of things to be discussed. Do the math. If you are planning to meet for thirty minutes and you have three topics, everyone is on notice to not spend more than ten minutes or so on the first topic. Knowing that you have multiple topics gives everyone permission to move on to the next. It encourages participants to respect each other's time and to stay on topic.

An agenda also puts participants at ease because they know what is coming. Members don't need to be distracted with worrying about when to raise a specific topic if they can see it's on the agenda for later. And if an agenda is shared in advance, it gives participants a chance to prepare in advance. People get time to quietly consider their thoughts and feelings. Depending on how far in advance an agenda is circulated, people can inform themselves about issues scheduled for discussion.

A good agenda demonstrates respect for everyone's time. For every hour spent in a meeting, multiply it by the number of people in the room, and then multiply that by the value of everyone's time. Meetings are costly. They are worth planning for.

FACILITATORS HELP THEIR GROUPS ACHIEVE

I define facilitation as *the art and practice of helping a group achieve its objectives.* When you are helping a group in a meeting, you are a meeting facilitator.

Notice that I say helping a *group* achieve *its* objectives, not *my* objectives. As a meeting facilitator, you don't work for just one person; you work for the group as a whole. And the word *helping* is broad on purpose. It means much more than standing in front of the room calling on people. It can include room setup, food, handouts, coaching leaders, coaching participants, tech support, follow-up documentation—in other words, anything that will help the group meet its objectives.

Facilitation is a combination of art and practice. A good facilitator—like a good artist—is a master of tried-and-true techniques applied in the artist's own style and differently in every situation. And, of course, you don't get good at facilitation without practice, discipline, and continual attention to improvement.

Although you can find an increasing number of career professional meeting facilitators in the world, you don't have to be a professional to facilitate meetings. Like all skills, the craft of meeting facilitation can be learned if the desire and discipline is strong enough.

You've likely heard many different names for a person who runs a meeting: boss, chair, mayor, speaker, prime minister, moderator, clerk, and facilitator, to name a few. These names have subtle distinctions based on the history and culture of their groups and also in their philosophies toward inclusiveness.

The boss of a group of subordinates might not care much about including perspectives of group members. The purpose of the boss's meeting might be to convey: "Here's how it's gonna be." Think "command-and-control" type of meeting leader. A boss might be inclusive and collaborative at times, but the point is, it's the boss's prerogative. The boss not only gets to make the final decisions but also to decide on the decision process. A board chair, speaker, mayor, or prime minister is obligated to follow an established decision-making process, which likely includes a requirement to hear minority opinions. Yet neutrality is not a requirement of the position, and the people who hold such positions are expected to push their own agendas. This type of meeting leader typically has a desired outcome in mind and tries to manipulate the process (hopefully within the rules) to get that outcome. Moderators, clerks (an old-fashioned term still used today by Quakers), and facilitators typically don't have a personal interest or premeditated outcome, and they work for active inclusion of all participants.

Each of these different styles of leading is completely legitimate based on its respective context and culture. Since this book is about collaborative decision-making, I am spotlighting the moderator/clerk/facilitator role, which is the style that maximizes collaboration and creativity. Even if you are not interested in the moderator/clerk/facilitator role—and you may not even be interested in collaboration—the stuff in this book won't hurt you! Many ideas here can help you be a better meeting leader, no matter your role or style.

GREAT FACILITATORS DO FOUR THINGS

When substance (the merits of one alternative over another) and process (the rules by which the merits get discussed and decided) are intertwined, the most powerful people manipulate the process and steer it toward their own desired outcomes. That's what's expected. That's what happens in Congress and in state legislatures and town councils across the country. Boardrooms too. The leader of the majority has a huge substantive stake in any decision *and* decides the process by which decisions are made. Yet when a group makes a deliberate separation between substance and process—puts the process functions in the hands of a neutral facilitator and leaves substance to the group members—it fosters fairness, collaboration, and creativity. When you separate substance from process, both are better.

In my experience the best meeting facilitators do the following four essential functions really well. Each of these may be done in a wide variety of ways with a wide variety of styles—go for it! But these are the basic functions:

> **Provide structure** in a number of ways. Good meeting facilitators are crystal clear on the purpose of the meeting and the purpose of each discussion. They design processes to match the purposes. They provide

and model meeting guidelines for group behavior. The good facilitator always knows where the group is in any discussion and what's next.

Encourage participation by creating a comfortable environment, setting a level playing field, and accommodating all personality types and styles. How the meeting is advertised, promoted, and publicized is critical. So is the timing and location. During the meeting, the best idea can come from anywhere and the good facilitator is always trying to bring that out. Attention to the details of inclusive participation results in creativity and innovation.

Move the group forward by seeing and capturing opportunities. The skilled facilitator is always looking to name common ground, recognize positive reactions, capture agreement, and sometimes even craft proposals—from a neutral perspective—to help the group get resolution. Even between meetings, the facilitator might be listening, nudging, or moderating negotiations toward agreement.

Reflect the group from a neutral perspective by providing summary statements of what the group has discussed, common themes, and/or agreements. Good facilitators "speak for the group" in a way that all group members appreciate. Written notes are also key to good facilitation, so the group is literally on the same page about what happened. Good facilitators give names to problems and solutions based on what they hear from the group.

INSIGHT: Closing Comments

Every chance we have to hear each other's perspectives is a chance to improve understanding and build the foundation for better decisions. And often, the most valuable comments come right at the end of a meeting or discussion. When people have become at ease with each other, they are more apt to speak from the gut. Make time for closing comments at the end of every meeting and encourage each person to share a reflection or a hope or concern going forward. The comments can be very quick if needed. Sometimes I say to a group, "These are going to take, like, ten seconds each." It also helps to set an order (after calling on a volunteer to start) so people can anticipate their turn. Speak your own closing comment *from* your heart. Take to heart the closing comments of others.

When you close every meeting by giving each person a chance to speak—even if super-brief—the group as a whole gets to see all the perspectives come together and unify at the end of a good meeting. It also provides one last chance for someone to give voice to something important.

WE CAN ALL FACILITATE

It's natural to think of meeting facilitation in the hands of a single person, since that's often how it looks. We may visualize one person at the front of the room who explains the agenda, keeps time, calls on people, reflects back what people are saying, and identifies themes. Yet there are many aspects to facilitation, some obvious and some behind the scenes. One need not be the official facilitator to do facilitation.

INSIGHT: Like a Restaurant Server

When I go to a restaurant, the server is my facilitator. They manage the process of my having an enjoyable meal. Yet behind the scenes, there are many people also facilitating my positive dining experience: the dishwashers, the managers, the cooks, the farmers, even those who printed the menus and built the building. These all come together in the facilitated experience of enjoying a meal at a restaurant. In a meeting, the facilitator stands at the front of the room like the server stands at the table, but there's a lot of other stuff going on behind the scenes.

And notice that a server doesn't tell me what to do. They're not a boss. Or a pilot. Rather they set up decision choices for me, they give advice if asked, but they let me lead and generally support me in achieving my objectives.

How the meeting goes is not all up to the person at the front. It is a shared responsibility. Group members are allowed to help. Maybe there's no designated leader at all and someone might say: "It seems to me that the reason we are here is to figure out how to get the best price for our potatoes this year. How about we start by hearing what John learned at the regional meeting, then hear everyone's ideas about what to do, and then decide on the best idea by taking a vote. Everyone OK with that?" That's facilitation. That was your meeting purpose and agenda in one sentence being presented to the group members for their consent.

Someone could follow up with something like "I think it would be good for Mary Alice to keep things on track, and I'm willing to take notes. And I hope we don't get bogged down in the past and complain about things we can't do anything about." That was a short version of clarifying roles and ground rules. Simply making these statements is an attempt to separate process from substance. The person who speaks up in this way is saying, "Let's decide a few process things first before we get into the substance," because they know that process underpinnings at the beginning will help the substance later.

If we are in a meeting that has a facilitator, an agenda, and ground rules, we can support the facilitator by being fully attuned to the agenda and ground rules and we can do our best to follow them. For me that often translates into exercising restraint. I help immensely if I am thoughtful and deliberate about when I talk and when I listen, and when my words are directly relevant to the current agenda item.

If you see that the agenda or ground rules are not being honored, point that out. Simply naming a violation opens the door for the facilitator to take action. You might say something like, "I just wanted to point out that we are already over time on this agenda item." Or you might say, "In my opinion the last comment was not in keeping with our ground rule that aggression is not OK." Just say what you see.

One last thing: If you are not the facilitator and the facilitator is doing a reasonably good job—even if handling things differently than you might—don't try to be the facilitator. "Process suggestions" are welcome when discussion of the group's process *is* the agenda topic. Process suggestions in the midst of a substantive discussion instantly blur the line between process and substance and both are likely to suffer. If you are not the facilitator and the facilitator is doing a bad job—I mean, really bad to the point where it's costly or destructive—call for a break and huddle with group leaders.

Many Hands Make Light Work

The primary job in any meeting is done by the person in charge of the process, often the designated facilitator. But that's not the only task that is important.

Space—Someone needs to secure the meeting space and set it up. Chairs and tables need to be arranged. Props such as projectors, screens, flip charts, and microphones need to be set up. Extra touches like tablecloths or fresh flowers all help.

Tech—If the meeting is online or uses special software or hardware, have someone focus on the tech aspects so the facilitator can focus on the people.

Food—Preparing the coffee or lemonade and baking cookies or muffins is all-important work. When food preparation is done with love and caring by members of the group, it makes for better meetings. If you're in a corporate setting, flowers add a nice touch. So can a whimsical image on your screen before the meeting starts. Anything that shows a common connection other than the business at hand will work to soften people up and remember that we are human.

Advance materials—Sending or posting agendas in advance, along with support documents or detailed instructions, is often helpful.

Note-taking—This job is best done by someone who is good at listening; it's a skill that good facilitators have. In my opinion, note-taking is facilitator training. Taking notes—just the important stuff—is a great way to practice a key aspect of good facilitation; that is, being able to figure out in a flash what's most important.

continued

Other jobs—Some groups appoint other roles, such as timekeeper, wall scribe, and greeter. Online roles include chat monitor, social media poster, and others. Some groups have special needs that require special work, such as taking care of kids so the parents can meet or translating spoken words into sign language.

When I was learning to be a meeting facilitator, I attended an in-person meeting with a very good meeting facilitator. I arrived five minutes early and she was waiting at the door. She greeted me, shook my hand, and said, "Coffee is over there, restrooms are down the hall, and we'll be sitting at this table."

A few more people arrived than she was expecting, so she hustled to set up two new "place settings": a set of handouts and a name card. She fetched a couple of chairs from the meeting room next door. She poured glasses of water for the two new people. She did all of these things herself rather than calling the hotel staff. She simply wanted to serve the people in the meeting as quickly and efficiently as possible. At the start of the morning break, she went over to the catering cart and took the plastic wrap off the food so that the meeting participants could eat quickly and efficiently. She showed people where to hang their coats and even had power strips set up under each table for people to plug in their laptops. She was the meeting facilitator—but did way more than just stand at the front of the room and call on people. I saw her do everything possible to make her meeting participants more comfortable, more efficient, and more productive. Watching her made me see how much I loved all aspects of helping groups make good decisions.

CHAPTER 12

From an Idea to a Decision

WHEN WE HAVE to make a group decision, it works well to figure out what we are deciding before we jump in. "What's the problem we are trying to solve?" or "What's the question we are trying to answer?" These are critical questions and if you don't take the time to answer them at the start, you will run into problems later.

It's impossible to overemphasize how important it is to get the problem right, yet many groups lose patience with problem definition. A person who likes action says, "Let's just get on with it! We know what the problem is!" What this person really means is, "*I* know what problem is." And chances are, they already have a particular solution in mind.

However, this person is seeing the problem and the solution from just one point of view. While "getting on with it" will satisfy their need to make progress, it will not likely serve the group. In fact, people fixing problems willy-nilly without collaborating first on defining the problems often results in more problems, more conflict, and huge inefficiencies.

THE PROPOSAL

When it's time for a group to actually start the decision-making process, it works well to have a written proposal. Proposals are boats that carry our ideas. Want to see if your idea floats? Write it up and send it around.

Let's say Jill is on a board of directors or town council. She takes an idea to Adeline, the group's chair (formal name for the leader of a board or council), about something for the group to enact. Adeline might say to Jill, "If you really

PROPOSALS HELP US TRY ON IDEAS.

want the group to consider this seriously, put your idea in writing. Say specifically what you want the group to decide." Jill's idea might not be fully formed yet. She might discuss it with others informally. But when the idea gets serious enough and defined enough for Jill to take to the group as a whole for action, it needs to be written down. Proposals are to groups as hypotheses are to scientists. Proposals and hypotheses provide a focus for the work, but they are not the answer until the process is complete.

Before you can start making decisions that lead to a grand resolution, you need to think about the order of things and put your proposal into phases accordingly. What needs to get decided first? What next? What can wait? Break decisions into pieces if you can, and consider the advantages of waiting to decide some pieces.

Once created and started on their journey, proposals are little vessels that we use to travel through the decision-making process. Proposals help us try on ideas. They are specific words that frame larger ideas. A proposal is something that an individual or a small group of people want a larger group of people to do—or think they want a larger group to do. Proposals help us explore what ideas might look like if turned into policy.

It may seem trivial but actually giving your proposal a name is very useful. For one thing, it helps when a proposal is carried forward from one meeting to another. When we see the name of a particular proposal on an agenda, we know what it's about, and we can trace it backward through the minutes of previous meetings. Another reason for naming, it requires critical thought about what the thing is actually about.

In addition to giving proposals names, some groups require that proposals have sponsors. The sponsor is a person (or in some cases a committee) who presents the proposal, answers questions about it, promotes it, and follows up on whatever is decided about it. The sponsor becomes the go-to person for that particular proposal.

It's important to remember that proposals and hypotheses often prove to be untenable. They may need alterations. They often fail. But even when ideas fail, they advance our work because they show us what won't work.

INSIGHT: To Name Is to Understand

When just the right words are used to name a proposal, situation, or perspective, it can bring instant relief and instant forward progress. Naming the proposal puts you over halfway to solving the problem. Name your proposal in a way that rings true. Don't avoid thinking hard about a difficult problem or conflict. Name it without judgment. Name it out loud so others can agree or challenge. Name it with honesty and integrity and be careful not to mislead. Be open to names suggested by others and open to renaming. People so often think they're saying the same thing and meaning the same thing but in reality, they are not in accord. Want to test if you are in accord? Agree on a name for whatever you are discussing.

MAKING IT TO THE TABLE IS NO SMALL THING

Collaborative groups want good ideas from anywhere, but not just any idea at any time. The time of the group as a whole is extremely valuable, and it's not OK for anyone to decide at any time that the group should turn attention to their idea. Back to Jill the group member and Adeline the group chair. Once Jill's proposal is ready for the group, she might request that it be added to the next meeting agenda. When Adeline hears Jill's agenda request she might persuade Jill to handle the issue another way or put off the issue to a future meeting or she might put it on the next agenda. *When* it gets onto the group agenda depends on other priorities for the group's time. As the group chair, Adeline is the agenda gatekeeper.

Controlling access to the agenda is a huge source of power. In many groups, setting an agenda is closely guarded by the majority or the chair or boss and is often used to limit opposition. Indeed, in many legislative bodies, the true power of the majority power lies in its ability to regulate what gets talked about and for how long, and what doesn't get talked about.

Among equals, deciding how to spend our time together should be a group decision. Or at least the group as a whole should decide how agendas get decided. It works well when every group member understands the agenda-setting process and has access to it. If you want to air all perspectives and share power, make it relatively easy for any new issue or idea to at least get a hearing. Some groups reserve a special time in every agenda where anyone can raise any issue—perhaps called an open forum—and then the issue might be sent to a committee or placed on a future agenda. The most inclusive groups have a well-publicized process for getting items onto a meeting agenda. If the agenda-setting process is not formalized or not widely understood in your group, it is surely limiting your creativity and your ability to make good group decisions.

In addition to setting the agenda, how decisions are made should be entirely visible and understood by all members of the group. Decision-making processes should be open and welcome to every decision-maker. That's what *Robert's Rules of Order*[29] and similar guidelines are all about—making sure a clear process is open to all.

Even if an item is on the agenda, most decision-making rules of procedure require that any motion—any proposal to

---

29 *Robert's Rules of Order* is widely used by municipal, nonprofit, and corporate boards across the country to guide smooth, orderly, and fairly conducted meetings.

be considered by the group—receive "a second" from a group member before it can be discussed. The idea is that for a group to seriously consider a proposal, at least two members need to think it's worthy of the full group's time. This is so the group cannot be dominated by a single person or an untested idea. If Jill cannot get at least one other person to think her idea is worthy of discussion, it doesn't get discussed and the group's time is saved.

I think that "getting a second" is generally a good practice. Here's the shortcut version if you're not so formal: "So Joe would like to talk about _____. Are there others who would like to talk about this as a group?" Pause. Look at everyone. If no one raises a hand, move on quickly to the next item.

Proposals often turn into written decisions. The process of understanding and debating and shaping the proposal together helps prevent conflict or inefficiencies later. Proposal development is literally making sure the group is on the same page.

One last thing about proposals. People like to know how they turn out, especially if invested. This is one reason why good record keeping—easily available to all members—is really helpful. Or if you are a leader and you asked people for input on a proposal, be sure to tell them later how it turned out.

THE DECISION-MAKING STEPS

When a group takes a vote, the motion is read aloud. The roll is called. The gavel goes down. That's the ceremony. Yet we know there is a lot more to it. The moment of voting may be a reverent one, but the truth is that significant work has been done prior to that moment. And significant work lies ahead before change actually happens. The test of the "goodness" of the decision has yet to come.

Think of decision-making like a wedding ceremony. It may seem as if a couple's decision to get married takes place at the altar, at the moment they recite their vows. We witness that decision with much ceremony and reverence at a precise moment in a sacred place. Yet we know that there were many steps preceding that moment, and there are many steps ahead. We know that those steps—both before and after the *I dos* at the altar—are built on a foundation of culture and tradition.

Another way to think of this is to consider a company that manufactures a product. Factories make products; groups make decisions. Like with products from a factory, group infrastructure supports the manufacture of a wide variety of decisions. Yet the *way* each decision gets made—what happens at each step—is adaptable.

Manufacturing steps include concept design, market research, product development, manufacture and assembly, sales and marketing, packaging and distribution, feedback, and refinement. Yet depending on the product, each of these steps is significantly adapted. The manufacture and sale of most products follow essentially the same steps—named above—but what happens at each step can differ depending on the features and volume of each product, and many other factors.

A company's infrastructure supports a variety of products because they use the same factory, same employees, and same equipment. Similarly, a group's infrastructure supports a variety of decisions with a variety of scale and stakes. This notion of adapting the scale of each decision step to the scale and complexity of the decision at hand is critical because many groups don't do it and it's a huge source of group inefficiency. The same basic steps should be followed for each decision, but the amount of effort applied in each step and the method applied to each step should vary considerably and should depend on the stakes and complexity of what you are trying to decide.

Whether you are a member of the Maine House of Representatives or part of a small group at a kitchen table, you can use the steps shown in the following diagram to making a good group decision. These steps assume that your group is established and has some basic group infrastructure in place such as common goals and basic decision-making rules.

These are the basic steps for collaborative decision-making. The amount of effort put into each step should be scaled in each case to the magnitude of the decision.

There is an order to the decision-making steps. If you are at any one of the steps in the diagram and things are not working, go back a step. That's the real value of this diagram. When your group is stalled or it seems like things are falling apart, this diagram tells you what step to go back to and redo. You might have to go all the way back to the framing. And that might be fine.

8. GROUP DECISION-MAKING STEPS

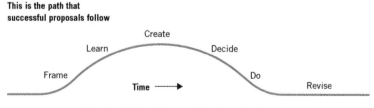

Notice the hill in the diagram. The steepest climb is learning and creating, trial and error, resolving tensions. The top of the hill is true creation of something new. That's the triumph. It's downhill from there. Deciding is actually easy once you have consensus on the creation; it's just a matter of writing it down or otherwise capturing it and checking that key players are in agreement. Implementing decisions—the doing—is a coast if it was set up by a good process. Then revise down the road.

Let's say a group's decision-making infrastructure is in place. The group has some version of by-laws and members and meeting guidelines and voting protocols. Someone has an idea for something new. Perhaps it's an adjustment to an existing thing. Perhaps it's a whole new thing. Perhaps it's something really big and could change the whole group. Perhaps it's teensy, but important to someone. Yet no matter the size of the idea, it can be run through these basic steps. And by the way, any idea can be scrapped at any stage along the way. That's not a bad thing. In fact, very few ideas should make it through all the steps, only the really good ones.

Let's take a closer look at each step:

STEP #1: FRAME

The frame provides the boundaries. It defines what is part of a decision and what isn't. Framing establishes the center line and the guardrails of a decision: What's the problem we're trying to solve? That's the center line, the thing that the new proposal is trying to make better. What is the scope of our reach? That is the guardrail that defines what's in and what's out of our authority.

Let's go to the factory floor of an imaginary company that makes beer and pretend that someone has an idea to make beer ice cream. The decision-making group might begin with questions like:

Are we talking just about ice cream? Or are we talking about maybe a whole suite of frozen beer products?

Do we have a budget? What are the limits on how much we plan to spend on market research or product development?

How long do we plan to spend exploring this? At what point will we make a decision?

Answers to these questions—even if rough answers that everyone agrees to—help the group define the focus and the boundaries. They frame the decision right from the get-go. They provide some sense of what's on track.

STEP #2: LEARN

This is where we gather all the information. We learn from experts and we learn from each other. Our goal here is to understand. This can be scaled to be as simple as a conversation—a check-in with someone before creating a solution—or it can be scaled big to include commissioned research, customer or stakeholder surveys, market analysis, focus groups, and other meetings to gather stakeholder input. This phase can also include prototyping, trying things on, and learning what doesn't work to solve the problem. In this phase we are also learning about each other—each other's interests—which will help us later when forming a solution that meets all our interests.

Sidebar: Science Trumps Intuition

We believe things to be true because our intuition tells us so and/or because science tells us so. Intuitive knowledge often comes quickly and is based on our direct and personal relationship with the thing that we are judging. It is a gut feeling. Scientific knowledge comes more slowly because, by definition, it has to be verifiable. Scientific methodology requires us to observe something repeatedly and see the same thing each time, or to do an experiment repeatedly and achieve the same results. Good science is way more costly to produce than ideas or opinions. Intuition is the far-easier path and we often take it just for that reason. Science is harder but, when available, it is a better basis for decisions. When science is at odds with intuition, it can be gut-wrenching.

If good science about the decision before you is available, use it. Even when the science points to inconvenient truths, is at odds with intuition, or seemingly impossible to accept, these are not excuses for denying or altering the truth. Good group decisions need the best knowledge available to the group so when good science exists, accept it and act on it.

STEP #3: CREATE

This is where the magic happens. This is where two or more ideas come together and create a new idea better than the single idea previously brought to the table. This is where we continue with the trial and error, refining our decision, creating our culture, and building support for it. Not only are we creating a decision (a solution, an answer, a thing), but we are also creating enduring support for the thing. We are creating belief in the thing we are making together. We are creating shared investment.

STEP #4: DECIDE

This step is where we actually make the decision, bring down the gavel, record the votes. Don't overlook this step. Put what you decided into writing. Date it. Say who was there.

DOCUMENTING DECISIONS PREVENTS FUTURE CONFLICTS AND INEFFICIENCIES.

The documentation acts as a snapshot in time that we can look back at to see who was there and what they decided. Documenting decisions prevents future conflicts and inefficiencies.

STEP #5: DO

Then you've got to do it. Good group decisions often name lead responsibilities and key deadlines. As part of the decision you make, you need to say who is going to do what by when. In my opinion, it is the decision makers—the board or the boss or the owners—who should take responsibility for getting implementation off to a good start. Give clear guidance and boundaries, and clarify roles from the start. Write these things into the text of the decision. Setting these expectations dramatically increases the chances that your decision will get done.

This step also requires individual responsibility and initiative. There's the riddle of the three frogs sitting on a log: One decided to jump off. How many frogs were left?

Well from what we know, three. *Deciding* to do something is not the same as *doing* it. If we don't do what we decided to do, the world doesn't change. We don't make progress. You have to actually jump to make an impact, to make ripples. Just thinking about stuff or even deciding stuff doesn't get stuff done.

INSIGHT: Being Human Is Not Just Thinking or Talking

We are not called human *thinkings* or human *talkings*, we are human *beings*. We have to *be* what we want to change in the world. We cannot intellectualize ourselves into making things better; we have to actually chop wood, carry water.[30]

Often, we shy away from doing things because we are afraid we cannot do them well. We are afraid of embarrassment. But it is better to take stumbling steps in the right general direction than take no steps at all. It is OK to do things poorly until we can do them well. It's called *practice*. Practicing gets good stuff done.

STEP #6: REVISE

Even though the decision has been made and even acted on, you're not done yet. No decision lasts forever. Revisions are needed after every decision. Plan on it. Build evaluation and revision into part of doing business. Groups that really care about the quality of their decisions evaluate how effective those decisions were. They want to see what impact they had—positive or negative—and they are willing to make changes in the future based on that feedback.

---

30   From a Buddhist saying, "Before enlightenment, chop wood, carry water. After enlightenment, chop wood, carry water."

There are several town and city councils in Maine that hire me to run annual goal-setting workshops, and we typically begin such a workshop by asking the question: "How did we do on last year's goals?" Not only do we answer this question, we also look for commonalities in the failures and the successes. We look for patterns and opportunities for systemic change. Many non-profit boards and corporate management teams also do regular reviews and make adjustments for the future. Combat and emergency units often do something called an "after-action," which is a formal debrief about something that went wrong and how to prevent it in the future. Many organizations regularly ask those most affected by the work of the organization—those most affected by the decisions—"How is it going?" More than a suggestion box in the front lobby, be deliberate and proactive and aggressive in seeking good information upon which to revise past decisions and make new ones.

Open to New Folks and New Ways

If we want the full benefit of newcomer participation in group decisions, we need to make sure they know how to participate fully in the process. Many groups have a newcomer orientation session or orientation materials. Fundamentals include expectations about participation, how to raise a concern or get items on the agenda, and where to go for various types of questions or requests. Some groups implement a mentoring or "buddy system" where newcomers are partnered up with veterans who show them the ropes at the start.

To periodically remind all group members about how things

are supposed to work, many groups have regular sessions to review and evaluate their decision-making process. Another technique is to rotate process-oriented jobs such as facilitation and recording minutes; if you have to do these things periodically it keeps you on your toes. A third technique is to occasionally invite outside experts to come and offer training, lectures, or workshops on group process techniques. Being exposed to new ways of doing things helps us evaluate our current methods.

In addition to "being open" in the sense that they are easily understood, group decision-making processes must also be open to change. A group's decision-making process is there to help the group achieve its purpose. If the process is not serving the group well, it should be changed so that it does.

To assess whether group processes are serving the group well, regularly ask those involved how it is working and how it could be improved. For example, some groups devote time at the end of each meeting for participants to make comments on how the meeting went. Some groups devote a portion of their annual retreat to examining issues of process. Some groups have a tradition that when officers retire, they write a brief report reflecting on how things could be improved.

We should not be afraid to look at ourselves and refine our processes. If we do not ask what could be improved, we are not likely to make improvements.

DON'T TRY TO FIGURE IT OUT ON THE FLY

As discussed in the previous section, frames are the first step to good decision-making for an important reason: They provide structure. With every new decision, we don't have to start from scratch. We already have something to build on. We have the group's organizational structure and rules of procedure, and we also have the array of all previous decisions, called precedent.

"We'll figure out the rules as we go" rarely works well if you want a good group decision. Decisions without advance framing are confusing, frustrating, and uncollaborative. It often works for the small group of people with the most power, but it never works for the group as a whole. Making up rules as you go helps those in power stay in power and get what they want, and marginalizes everyone else. If you are a leader who truly wants collaborative decisions, establish rules for a level playing field before the game begins.

IF YOU ARE A LEADER WHO TRULY WANTS COLLABORATIVE DECISIONS, ESTABLISH RULES FOR A LEVEL PLAYING FIELD BEFORE THE GAME BEGINS.

It is fairer and more efficient to establish rules and framing before tensions start then after you are in the thick of it. Once you have a conflict on the table, then any discussion about rules for resolving the conflict will be tainted by each person considering how any proposed rule will affect their stake in that particular conflict. Those with the most power will put rules into play that will help them get their way. The fair approach is for each team to agree to the rules before taking the field.

Framing doesn't just provide fairness; it provides efficiency and prevents conflict. It provides shared understanding among everyone about what's going to happen next. For example, an employee at a restaurant wants to start a recycling program. They're concerned about all the cardboard boxes that go into the garbage and wish the boxes could be recycled instead. They raise the idea with their boss who tells them: "Thanks for thinking about how to make things better around here. Good job. If you really want to advance this, write up why you think we should do this and then do a little research. Find out where we can get cardboard recycled, how it would work, and how much it would cost. Also, get some input from other employees. Ask them if they would be willing to make the extra effort to separate the cardboard. When you have that information for me, I will take it to the owners and ask them for a decision." There, decision framed. The boss could have said, "Sounds good. Take a next step on that." With no framing or boundaries, the restaurant employee might have ordered a dumpster or hired a recycling contractor or any number of steps that the boss didn't anticipate. Because the boss framed the next step, the people involved had shared expectations.

Here's another example: The city of Westbrook, Maine, acquired some land known as the Westbrook City Forest and wanted to make a decision about how to use it. The city council asked the city's Recreation Committee to learn the possibilities of how the land might be used, assess the recreational needs of the city, and to gather public input, then develop a recommendation to city council on how the land should be used. A deadline was established and a budget was provided. That's framing.

BEWARE OF BEING TOO CASUAL

Sometimes we get tricked into thinking that casual is fine. We may think that we don't need formalities like rules or agreements or proposals or that we don't need those things written down. We all know that person who

SOMETIMES WE GET TRICKED INTO THINKING THAT CASUAL IS FINE.

says things like, "Ah, come on. I'm trustworthy. We're buddies, you and I." And they make it seem all about the relationship. Of course, there are people who really believe in relationships, and if you have good, solid, trustworthy relationships among your fellow decision makers, then you don't need to write as much down. That is a lovely ideal, and it works well in a lot of groups. But I'm telling you that it goes astray the moment the relationship goes astray. When relationships go bad or even just drift apart for no bad reason, it's pretty handy to be able to fall back on written rules, agreements, or proposals.

When we don't have processes or agreements written down and then a conflict erupts, the outcome is most likely to favor the stronger player, regardless of what the parties agreed to. Framing and proposals are really conflict prevention techniques and they also provide for greater inclusivity and tend to level the playing field for all participants.

Many groups are casual about beginning the process of giving form and shape to an idea. For instance, a group might take up an issue spontaneously, without notice to stakeholders. This works well if you are "in the room" and don't actually want too many people to know about or participate in the decision, but it doesn't work well if you are "outside the room" yet have a stake. And it also doesn't work well for organizations who want to make truly collaborative decisions.

I'm not saying that ideas can't be talked about in hallways or coffee shops or bars or kitchen tables. That's how ideas get born and solutions get generated. Yet when a group, as a group, begins to take up an issue for deliberation—and if they want to invite the best available thinking—the group should have a formal start to the decision-making process and let all stakeholders know about it.

Groups may also run the risk of being too casual about finalizing and formalizing decisions. Meetings are often adjourned with the leader saying something like, "OK then, I guess we're all set." And others in the room are thinking, "Wait. What do you mean we're all set? What did we just decide?"

When the leader says, "We're all set," they probably have an idea in their head of what just got decided, but chances are, their version of the decision does not match what others in the group think. Without formally acknowledging that, yes, we just made a group decision, and then writing it down for all to see or stating it for all to hear, conflict and inefficiency are sure to follow.

Sometimes decision-making might be spontaneously started and then resolved in the same meeting. Yet wherever possible, highly collaborative groups want to give advance notice of an upcoming decision and spread a decision-making process over at least two or more meetings. Advance notice gives all stakeholders a heads up. If we want collaborative decisions, we actually want all stakeholders involved, even if we think they might be against us. And spreading a decision-making process out over two or more meetings gives everyone a chance to consider the proposal and alternative proposals between meetings.

NO BACK ROOMS

It is frustrating to be a decision maker in a group and not understand how the decisions are made. For one thing, groups that shield their decision-making processes are limiting access to a subset of decision makers. If someone can't see how the process works and where they are supposed to plug in, they are not apt to participate. The group misses out on their contributions. If we are expected to know our way around a place, it is helpful to be given a map.

In many organizations, decision-making processes are intentionally shielded from the "rank and file" members to protect the authority of those in power. It is a tried-and-true technique as old as the hills. However, hidden passages into back rooms and secret handshakes compromise our ability to make good group decisions. Non-transparent decision-making shuts out good ideas and closes off opportunities. Good group decisions rely on open processes so all stakeholders can see how to participate effectively.

If you want real inclusion, it's not enough for processes to be passively transparent. That's when you have fulfilled your legal obligation for transparency and nothing else, for the most part. To be proactively transparent is not only that; it's going an extra step and reaching out to your audience in ways that you know will work for them. Want to reach a target audience? Use words that they use in places where they go. Proactively explain why this or that is important to your group and why you are doing this or that.

Two clients of mine, each manufacturing plants, have established formal community advisory panels made up of government, business, and nonprofit leaders. They hire me to facilitate regular meetings of these panels for two specific purposes: 1) so that plant managers can convey accurate information about their operations to the public and 2) so community leaders can bring up questions or rumors before they get out of hand. "It's insurance," one of the plant managers told me once. The proactive transparency and communications channel is a hedge against future disaster.

Benefits of Including All the Employees

A family-owned company came to me for help with strategic planning. This company had been built on a long tradition of community engagement and trust. Deals were made with handshakes and the two owners made many decisions based on gut feelings. As the two owners approached retirement, they wanted a smooth transition. They wanted their customers to maintain a high level of trust in the company. They wanted their employees, especially the new leaders, to know the handshake deals and the unwritten rules. They had this idea that they wanted to go to a mountain resort to talk about it.

They had an excellent instinct, but when it came time to actually write the agenda for meeting in the mountains, they were lost. As with most of my clients at the very start of an engagement, I helped them clarify what it was that they really wanted to achieve. Turns out it was more than just wanting to talk about the transition. I helped them tease out four specific objectives, one of which was a shared understanding of how the transition was going to work. They also wanted to build team unity. They wanted to take stock of their current situation: who they were as a company and what their strengths and weaknesses were. And they wanted to establish a general sense of strategic direction that was understood and supported by all.

I helped them put those things (their meeting objectives) into a logical order and make an agenda for a two-day meeting. I also helped them decide who should participate. This was a company of about forty employees. There were the two owners, the executive team, some middle managers, and all the other employees.

continued

Based on the objectives and our discussions, they decided that everyone, every single employee, would be invited to the meeting.

The owners shut down their business and brought the whole crew to the mountain resort for the two-day facilitated meeting. Everyone was treated with respect and encouraged to contribute. The meeting helped everyone in the company understand how things worked and who did what. And because they had meals together and laughed together, they got to know each other in new ways. They felt a tremendous sense of belonging and a sense of shared enthusiasm for their future. Back in the office, day-to-day work went more smoothly and more cheerfully. Senior and middle managers were better equipped to work things out peacefully because the relationships were even stronger than before and because everybody had a shared sense of what they were working toward.

This company was so pleased with the result of this two-day retreat that they hired me to help them the following year and the year after that and the year after that. And having worked with them for several years, I can see how their investment has paid off. For one thing, it's been a smooth transition. This is the main thing they wanted to achieve. The two owners who first hired me have now completely retired and ownership is in the hands of a new generation of leaders doing things in new ways—while retaining the old trust. Second, the company is more profitable as a result of their investment in good group decisions. They are more profitable because they have decreased expenses by reducing redundancies. They've been able to do this by being more transparent across departments and across the whole company, and where they see opportunities to do things more efficiently, they take them. This requires individuals to be adaptable and fine with changing jobs in service to the company's greater goals.

They work smarter and more streamlined because they take time every year—whether they need it or not—to look at how they work together and how they can do things better.

A third result of this investment is what the leaders report as a corporate cultural shift. People get along with each other better and feel better about the company's future and their role in it. There is a wonderful sense of shared purpose among the employees of this company. It is a sought-after place to work. Morale is high. Their customers can see and feel this corporate culture of positivity.

A fourth benefit of their investment: innovation. This company has had some breakthroughs, moved into some new markets, and done some things in radically different ways. Such new ways were invented and developed in group meetings like the retreats. And they stay innovative by continually asking all employees for ideas on how to make things better. The leaders of this company know that the best ideas can come from anywhere at any time. So they ask everyone all the time.

CHAPTER 13

Key Questions
in Any Process

SOMETIMES IT WORKS well to jump headlong into decision-making as a group, especially if you are a seasoned team trained to work in a hurry. Firefighters arriving at a fire scene make group decisions very efficiently. Yet for non-emergency situations where we have choices about how much time and effort to spend on decision-making, it pays to consider the following questions at the outset. This is the key to making group decisions efficiently: matching the decision-making process to the scale of the problem to be solved or the question to be answered.

WHAT'S THE PROBLEM?

We've likely all been in meetings where the discussion is moving along and people seem engaged, but in fact, some in the group are confused. Lively conversation may continue, but beneath the surface confusion is building and leading to frustration. Finally, someone says, "Wait a minute. What is the question we are trying to answer?" or "What's the problem we are trying to solve?" It's almost always a variation of one or both of these questions. In other words, one or more people have lost track of the group's focus and lost sight of what they're working toward.

Over half the work of solving a problem is defining it. Many times I have seen groups come up with a great solution to the wrong problem. They might have got lucky and actually solved another problem. Or they might have solved an imagined problem.

For example, I worked with a city where the downtown business owners said they were losing money because the city did not provide enough downtown parking spots. They pushed the city council to change the zoning and issue bonds to borrow money to build a parking lot. But a research project

OVER HALF THE WORK OF SOLVING A PROBLEM IS DEFINING IT. revealed that employees of downtown businesses were parking closest to the stores and taking all the best spots. The problem wasn't that the city did not provide enough parking spots. If they had built a solution to fix that problem, they would have invested in more parking but would not have solved the real problem. The real problem was that not enough parking spaces were available to customers. And that problem could be solved by requiring employees to park a block away. That problem called for a management fix rather than an infrastructure fix.

The word *solve* comes from the Latin word *solvere*, which means to loosen or break into parts. When we solve a problem, we untangle it from other pieces. In a group decision-making setting, a good way to do this is to write out a problem statement, which breaks down the problem in words for all to see. This discipline is similar to the scientific discipline of writing a hypothesis, or the legal discipline of writing a complaint. Before we tear into the work of resolution and decision-making, we have to make sure we understand what it is we are trying to resolve. Here's another example.

A church board of trustees was concerned about declining attendance at Sunday school. The three-year downward trend was clear and, for some, alarming. A meeting was called to address the issue. One person immediately suggested sending a letter to the entire congregation encouraging kids to attend Sunday school. Another suggested the time of Sunday school be altered slightly to make it easier for families with kids. Another suggested changing the Sunday school curriculum. Another suggested joining two classes together to make for a fuller class.

Then a man said, "Wait a minute. What's the problem we're trying to solve?"

"Well," someone said matter-of-factly, "not as many kids are attending Sunday school."

"How is that a problem?" asked the man. It was a courageous question against the grain of assumption. His question was met with accusatory looks that conveyed thoughts of "What's the matter with you? Are you anti-Sunday school?"

People tried to answer the man's question, but in every instance, he asked again, "And how is that a problem?" He was peeling back layers of information, like layers of an onion, to arrive at deeper understanding.

The man kept asking, and the others kept providing answers,

all of which were based on the assumption that high Sunday school attendance was simply part of the church fabric and the church's mission. After some time they hauled out the church's mission statement and found that it said nothing about Sunday school but rather spoke in general terms about providing education. "If our goal is education," the man said, "maybe the problem is that Sunday school has become outdated. Are there more effective ways to do education?"

He continued: "The problem is that we are not fulfilling our potential in providing education to young members of our congregation." All agreed with this reframed statement of the problem.

Once the issue was stated in this way, the trustees began to look at all the ways they were currently providing education to young people and all the ways that they could. They discussed camping trips, plays, talent shows, Friday night pizza for teens, and getting elementary-age kids to help with ushering.

As they came up with creative solutions to the real problem, the fact that Sunday school attendance was slipping became a minor issue. In fact, when they attacked the real problem and instituted a wide variety of solutions, Sunday school attendance actually crept back up because the kids developed camaraderie and simply wanted to be with each other.

In this example, the definition of the problem was expanded thus unlocking wider creativity on the larger, and more relevant, problem. In the next example, the definition of the problem gets narrowed, thus unleashing focused creativity on the actual problem.

A town resident was deeply concerned about unleashed dogs coming in her yard and chasing the squirrels, and then one day a dog actually caught a squirrel and it was very disturbing to her.

She went to a meeting of her town council where she complained and proposed a rule that all dogs must be on leashes. When she was told that such a rule already existed, she argued that the fines should be higher and there should be more enforcement. She threatened to petition town hall to raise taxes and hire more police to address the menacing problem of loose dogs, since she was sure that the problem was related to how the town handled loose dogs. Naturally, with that view of the problem, she sought to change how the town handled loose dogs.

Then a neighbor asked, "Do you know whose dog it is that comes in your yard and chases squirrels?" She replied that she did. "Have you talked to the dog's owner?" the neighbor asked compassionately. She had not. "Isn't the real problem," the neighbor suggested, "that *a particular* dog comes into your yard and chases squirrels?"

With a new, more circumscribed definition of the problem, the woman was able to muster the courage to confront the dog's owner and talk things through. They talked about tying the dog up, they talked about fences, and they talked about muzzling the dog. They came to understand each other's perspective and arrived at a solution whereby the dog would not be allowed to run free into the lady's yard except after dark when the squirrels were in trees asleep.

In both of these examples, when individuals took time to define the true problem, creative solutions came easily. Not only that, the solutions squarely addressed the problem at hand. Working on solutions unrelated to the actual problem can create more problems, confusion, and huge inefficiencies for lots of people.

Finally, when trying to define a problem, it works well to get input from those closest to the problem. Often a group of leaders—such as a board of directors or group of bosses—think that they know what problem the frontline workers face, and they instruct them to solve that problem. For example, the owners of a stadium believe that long lines outside the stadium are due to people not getting through the ticket-taking staff fast enough. The ticket-takers are the problem, they conclude. So they tell the stadium manager to add more ticket-taking staff. If the owners had asked the ticket-takers what their ideas were for getting more people into the stadium faster, they would have gotten the answer, "Print the barcode on both sides of the ticket so we never have to fumble to find the right side for scanning. That would speed things way up without adding staff."

One more suggestion: When defining a problem, it's very helpful to imagine what things would look like if the problem were solved. What numbers would we expect to see change if the problem were solved? Many groups are extremely deliberate about this and establish measurable objectives or key performance indicators that they expect to improve. For instance, I worked with Casco Bay Lines, the island ferry service in Portland, Maine. When they decided on a schedule change, they expected customer satisfaction to go up and expenses would go down as a result of the change. And they put in place provisions to collect numeric data and monitor for these outcomes.

WHO DOES WHAT?

A huge source of discontent and conflict in groups comes from misunderstanding who has what role. Someone may think they are a decision maker but actually they are just an advisor. Who has a vote and who has input? Who in the end will make the final decision? All of us? Most of us? Just one of us? Deciding at the beginning who will decide at the end helps your group design an appropriate process, and it lets everyone know what to expect from the start. Mismatched processes and mismatched expectations are huge sources of inefficiency and conflicts in groups.

In the case of an employee who wants to recycle cardboard, their boss tells them, "I will take it to the owners and ask them for a decision." Perfect. From that moment on, the employee doesn't need to worry that a recycling program will be their decision or their boss's decision. The employee has been told who will decide.

It's important to be deliberate about how each decision will be made and what each person's role will be in each case. A one-size-fits-all approach is rarely best. Sometimes a smaller committee is best; sometimes an individual can do the job. For each decision, your role might be different. A popular project management tool called a RACI chart identifies four different roles that I might play for any given decision: responsible, accountable, consulted, and/or informed. Take the time to be clear on who is playing what role at all times.

Sometimes groups lay out a multi-phase process where roles change: "We are asking a particular small group to decide this, but if they can't all agree, then the general manager will decide." This works really well in cases where there is a lot of tension or disagreement. The large group is empowering a small group to solve the problem or answer the question with a unanimous decision, but if they can't,

MISMATCHED PROCESSES AND MISMATCHED EXPECTATIONS ARE HUGE SOURCES OF INEFFICIENCY AND CONFLICTS IN GROUPS.

there is a backup plan. There is a way for a decision to get made and for the group to move forward in spite of disagreement that takes too long to resolve.

Another strength of the backup plan is that it serves as motivation to the small group. Let's say a school district gets awarded money from the state for running the school. Some of this money was budgeted for a new front office, but there's disagreement on how the new front office should be configured. However, if this disagreement doesn't get resolved and if the money doesn't get spent by the end of the fiscal year, the money goes back to the state and how it gets spent will be decided by state employees rather than by school leaders.

WHO DECIDES?

We tend to apply overly complex processes to small decisions or overly simple processes to large decisions. We ask a large group to make a short-lived decision that affects just a few. Or we allow a small group to make an intergenerational decision that affects millions.

As we've discussed in Chapter 2 and diagram 4, there is a range of ways that groups make decisions. Sometimes, one person decides on behalf of everyone else in the group. Other times, most of the group decides for everyone. And sometimes, every group member participates in the decision. But the *one decider*, *majority rule*, and *I agree* methods simply describe the middle and end points of a complex spectrum of all the ways groups can make decisions.

FLAT FOR PLANNING, STACKED FOR DOING

Deciding what things should be like in the future—*planning*—is well suited to a flat decision-making structure; that is, where several decision makers are equal and all fully participate. Consensus decision-making is at this end of the spectrum. As a rule, the longer and wider the reach of the plan, the broader and flatter the decision-making structure should be.

Deciding how to implement plans—*doing*—is better suited to a hierarchical decision-making structure; that is, roles and responsibilities are stacked on each other. There is a chain of command and accountability up and down the ladder. As a rule, the more expeditious and short-lived a decision is, the better it is to delegate it to an individual or another group within a hierarchy.

For example, on the field of battle, the commander decides, everyone obeys, and plans are swiftly implemented. Back home in the United States Senate, the foreign policy that guides the battle is made more slowly and with a wide array of input.

Deciding on the design of a new town hall—a building expected to last hundreds of years—should involve many stakeholders. Deciding what paper to use in the photo copier in the new town hall is a single-person decision. Decisions with a limited sphere of impact are good for single deciders or small groups, but when a decision affects hundreds of people—or thousands or millions of people—then hundreds, thousands, or millions of people should be involved.

For each decision, first determine the type of decision: Is it more of a planning-type decision or more of an implementation-type decision? Will it have long-term impact or short-term impact? Will it affect a lot of people or just a few? Apply a decision-making method appropriate to the nature of the decision. Some issues get sent to a single decider. Some issues go into a majority-rule process. And some issues are deemed to have such long and wide affect that a consensus-building process is set in motion.

The point is to be deliberate. The method should be stated out loud or presented in writing so everyone knows in advance how things will be decided. This is important because it provides equal opportunity for all participants, and it provides a solid foundation for when things get tough (so the group does not slide into debate about *how* to decide a tough issue).

Tree of Collaboration

If you want your group to be both organizationally collaborative and individually decisive, you might try a *tree of collaboration* rather than a *chain of command*.

The trunk of the tree of collaboration represents the core reasons why the group exists. The trunk is the group's mission, values, and strategic direction. Trunk-type decisions are made slowly with lots of people involved.

Big branches are the major areas of activity, each governed by a different yet connected group. Smaller branches are programs, agencies, divisions, and departments. The twigs are small teams. And then there are the leaves—the frontline workers—where many decisions get made by individuals.

We trust people throughout the organization (the leaves) to make decisions on behalf of the organization because they are connected to the mission, values, and strategic plan. Each frontline decision maker can be trusted to make aligned decisions.

In a *chain of command*, each link is connected in a line to another, yet each link is physically separate. The links rattle. In the tree of collaboration, the same sap runs through the whole tree. Each leaf and bud are genetically connected, seamlessly, with no gaps.

Common meals in my cohousing community are done by a tree of collaboration. The basic rules about common meals (the trunk) are established by the group as a whole. Whether written or not we have neighborhood values such as including everyone, sharing, and cleaning up after yourself. Main branches are things like shopping, cooking, cleaning, scheduling, and finances. These branches all have their own rules and culture yet they are all connected to the same core values. The little twigs and the leaves are the community members who rearrange the chairs, do the dishes, and put away the pots. We the members make hundreds of tiny little decisions on behalf of the group, yet these decisions are all attached to our core principles. As a group we are happy for most decisions to be made by individuals—at the leaf level—because we know that each leaf is connected to a branch of the tree. And to take the analogy just one step further, when we approach a tree we see the leaves first. The infrastructure of the twigs, branches, and trunk is hidden by the foliage.

9. TREE OF COLLABORATION

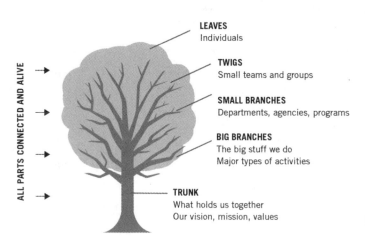

LEAVES
Individuals

TWIGS
Small teams and groups

SMALL BRANCHES
Departments, agencies, programs

BIG BRANCHES
The big stuff we do
Major types of activities

TRUNK
What holds us together
Our vision, mission, values

ALL PARTS CONNECTED AND ALIVE

Different from the
CHAIN OF COMMAND
where the links rattle

USING DECISION CRITERIA

Years ago, the Maine Department of Labor was faced with having to close some of its CareerCenters, which are places where unemployed people can go for job training and to learn about available jobs. How was the department going to decide which ones to close and which to leave open?

When there are no decision criteria in this type of setting, politics tend to prevail. That is, CareerCenters in areas with the least amount of political power would be closed and those with the most political power would remain open.

Without decision criteria, decisions are based on the personalities and views of the most powerful people. Decisions are made not based on what is best for the group as a whole but rather based on fear of retaliation, such as fear of losing future funding, fear of losing support for future issues, or fear of losing valuable relationships. In cases where the decision will result in some people winning and some people losing, the group is better served if decision criteria are established in advance of having to make actual win-lose decisions.

In this example, high-level Department of Labor officials convened all the CareerCenter managers and asked the group to establish decision criteria. I was the facilitator. They came up with a list of decision criteria such as cost savings, coverage area, and needs of the population served. Then they proceeded to weight the criteria. They decided that cost savings was worth seventy points, coverage area was worth twenty points, and needs of the population served was worth ten points.

They established the weighted decision criteria *before* beginning to discuss actual CareerCenters. Then they simply applied the criteria to each CareerCenter and added up the points.

Similar processes are often used when a group has to make a hiring decision. After the job interviews, members of the hiring committee rate each candidate on predetermined criteria. Yet a group rarely gives over its entire decision-making authority to a weighted criteria process. After all, there are always other considerations, and the criteria and weights are never perfect. In the case of hiring someone for instance, there is no scientific accounting for good vibes or gut instinct. It can be helpful, however, for a group to establish advance decision criteria and do some scoring even if for no other reason than to serve as a starting place for discussion. Just the process of developing criteria deepens the group's understanding of the nature of the outcome that they seek.

INSIGHT: If You Feel Stuck

When it seems like your group is stuck and cannot decide something, you can at least decide *how* you will decide. Name a next step that moves you in the direction of eventual agreement. Make a plan for a future discussion and vote, send it to a small group or committee with a specific charge, or name a third-party decider.

For instance, "We can't agree on the floor plan for the new building, so we're going to spend time on this topic at our next meeting, hear both sides, and vote. Is that OK with everyone?" If everyone can agree on how the thorny issue will be decided, that's progress toward agreement. When we send something to a committee or even to a person with something like, "Let's ask Louise and let her decide," we are making a decision about how to decide.

continued

> When diplomats or politicians spend time on meeting arrangements, seating plans, and the details of meeting agendas—the conditions under which the parties agreed to meet—they are really deciding how they will decide. They are taking what looks like tiny steps but they are actually building agreement.

WHAT'S THE RUSH?

Groups often struggle with what issues to spend their time on, what to put off, what to delegate, and how much effort to devote to each issue. Absent some deliberate advance planning, groups end up spending time on things that appear to be most urgent to those with the most power. And this often results in the most important things not getting done. In his book *The 7 Habits of Highly Effective People,* Stephen Covey explains the trade-offs of spending time on urgent things versus important things and encourages us to consider these trade-offs as we plan our time.

As each issue comes to light, ask, "What is the urgency of deciding this issue?" Sometimes when we take the time to ask this question and when we are thoughtful about the order in which we take up issues, the issues disappear. Another thing that happens when we ask this question carefully: We see that issues can be broken into pieces, with one piece needing to be decided right away but that the whole thing doesn't need to be decided with the same urgency.

Also ask, "How big of an issue is this? What is its potential impact?" To determine an issue's potential impact, we need to look at the number of individuals affected, the depth of penetration of the impact, and the length of time that the impact will last. The total impact is determined by multiplying these three factors together, at least in your imagination if you don't have numbers. For instance, an issue that affects just one person just a little bit for just a little while does not have much total impact.

1O. DECISION IMPACTS FAR AND WIDE

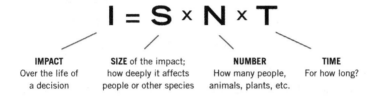

IMPACT	SIZE of the impact;	NUMBER	TIME
Over the life of a decision	how deeply it affects people or other species	How many people, animals, plants, etc.	For how long?

Ideally, decisions with a large impact are worthy of a large decision-making process. For a decision likely to affect thousands of people for many years into the future, we want a robust process. For a decision likely to affect just a few people for a year or two, the process can be simpler.

Here's the thing: Groups expand processes to fill all available time and space. This is why it makes sense at the start of a decision-making process to determine, at least in a rough way, the scope of impact and the proportional scope of the decision-making process. Limit the time and space right from the get-go to guard against your group wasting time on small stuff and perhaps even creating problems where they didn't otherwise exist.

HOW FAR TO TAKE THIS?

There's no need to decide any more than what's necessary. The best things are always built in stages—even in the case of dramatic change. Even what seems like miraculous change actually results from many small steps. When we take small steps, we learn as we go and we adjust as we learn.

Make use of pilot projects, test cases, and trial runs. Make commitments incrementally. Try things in small stages before acting out on big stages. Fail fast and fail cheap, as the saying goes. Let's say a group member asks, "What's the most we can do to achieve our objective?" Make sure you also ask, "What's the least we can do?" It is better to take a small step in what we know is the right direction than to take a large step in what might be the wrong direction.

"We did the best we could with the time, tools, and information that we had." It's so great when you can say this. And notice the second word. We *did* something, even with limited resources. When groups get stuck, they often fail to achieve anything because they don't have enough time, tools, or information to achieve everything. They can't make *as good* or *as big* a decision as they would like, so they make no decision at all. Yet in reality, most groups *never* have enough time, tools, or information to make perfect decisions. The trick is to do the best you can with what you have rather than stay stuck while waiting or wishing for more information or resources. And "the best we could" does not mean "the most we could." It's more about quality than quantity.

If you can see that you are starting to fall short of a deadline, you might honor the deadline anyway but perhaps with a less complicated product or service. Pushing off a deadline once or twice for good reason is fine, but repeatedly missing deadlines to achieve perfection just results in missed deadlines and stalled projects. Honoring deadlines with smaller achievements is at least progress in the right direction and helps everyone learn along the way. When others fall short of deadlines or other expectations, try to give them a break. One's ability to achieve is always related to one's blessings and burdens.

CHANGE THE POLICY OR
CHANGE THE PRACTICE?

If it becomes apparent that people are behaving contrary to an agreement, step one is to point out how the behavior is contrary to an agreement (people may simply not know). If contrary behavior continues, there are two choices: 1) enforce the agreement by imposing consequences on violators or 2) formally change the agreement to be in line with the behavior. Things change and sometimes agreements need to change. That's fine. For example, a Maine kids camp sends young summer campers on multi-day canoe trips where they sleep in tents for a few days. Sometimes it rains. The written rule was that no tent should be brought back to camp wet. In practice, this proved impossible and caused a lot of tension. And besides, the gear manager back at base camp dried all the tents upon return anyway. So they changed the written rules.

If you see that practices of people in your group are out of line with the policies of your group, and enforcement doesn't make sense because the policy doesn't make sense, change the policy. It's not OK to ignore what you see and let group policies become more and more irrelevant.

CHAPTER 14

How to Fuel Creativity

"IF AT FIRST the idea is not absurd, then there is no hope for it." Widely attributed to Albert Einstein, this quote has special significance for all of us wanting good group decisions. For real creativity to occur, people have to feel safe. We have to create an environment where individuals feel free to propose any idea no matter how absurd.

Framing, as we discussed earlier, is one way to make people feel safe because people like knowing what's expected, the parameters of the activity. Meeting facilitation is another way we provide safety, because its structure provides comfort. When someone is in charge and there's an agenda, people

WHEN WE FEEL SAFE, WE'RE NOT AFRAID TO TAKE RISKS; WE FEEL AS IF THERE'S A NET UNDERNEATH OR A FENCE ALONGSIDE.

know what to expect. That helps some people feel safe. If I'm a participant, it's especially helpful for me to trust the facilitator, to trust that they are not going to waste my time, not embarrass me, or not let anyone disrespect me. When we feel safe, we're not afraid to take risks; we feel as if there's a net underneath or a fence alongside.

Here's an example of brainstorming where people felt safe. I ran a meeting for a foundation to improve how college scholarships are promoted to high school students. When we began brainstorming, people tossed out their thoughts. First, someone suggested that the foundation increase its direct contact with high school students. Then came the idea of donating bulletin boards to high schools, so at least each school would have a place to physically post the foundation's materials. And then came the idea that every bulletin board should somehow be branded; perhaps have the foundation's name on the frame with a website promoting the scholarships. Then came the idea that the foundation could donate multiple branded bulletin boards to each school to use however they wanted. In this way, ideas got built upon ideas and the group came up with a solution that no one of them had on their own.

It's important to withhold criticism during brainstorming. Imagine in the above example if someone had shot down the ultimate solution in the early stages. Criticism not only risks killing the current idea, but many subsequent ones. We think, "If that's going happen to me, I'm not even going to share my idea."

Another safety-building and creativity-generating technique is to give up ownership of ideas so that the group can criticize the ideas without criticizing the people who offered them. In the above example, when the second person offered a new idea, the first person didn't get defensive and say, "Well that's not really what I was thinking." In high-functioning groups, a particular person's vision for an idea doesn't stay with the idea once the person gives their idea to the group. Ideas belong to the group to criticize, delete, or build on however they want.

Also, just because your group can't see exactly where you are headed, don't let that stop you from taking the next step. Let that be enough for now. Take a step. Let go of needing to know everything. It's like walking in the dark with a hanging oil lantern. It casts a circle of light on the ground around me, and I can only see so far. I can't tell what's beyond the circle out there in the dark. Yet when I move forward, the light moves with me and I can see my next step.

IF YOU SEEM STUCK WITH UNCERTAINTY, ASK, "WHAT'S THE LEAST WE NEED TO KNOW TO TAKE THE SMALLEST STEP WE CAN?"

Nothing breeds success like success, goes the popular saying. Achieving small goals provides motivation for achieving bigger goals. When it looks like your group is underachieving, or when morale is down, establish some achievable goals and see what it feels like to win. Boost morale. Move the bar back up later.

Structure Supports Creativity

Decision-making structure consists of things like rules, agendas, mandates, and plans. When we use these things to frame our choices, we are freed up to focus on the substance of our work. When an elementary school teacher assigns seats in the classroom, they're not taking away the students' freedom to make choices, they are relieving the students of the burden of that particular decision thus allowing them to focus on more important things. The students could have used a lot of energy and created a lot of drama deciding who gets to sit next to who, but since the teacher provides that structure, their energy goes to art and math and reading.

continued

Establishing a firm structure allows maximum creativity within the structure. Knowing there's a container provides safety and encourages risk-taking. Lack of structure fosters anxiety and encourages caution. Lack of structure causes inefficiency in many ways.

Establish decision-making rules in your group—even if super-simple and high-level—and make it someone's responsibility to enforce them. Make sure everyone understands and agrees to the rules before you decide other things. When your group takes up a complex decision, break it into pieces with a timeline for deciding each piece (timelines are another form of structure). Focus on one piece at a time. Be bold in enforcing your structure—and then go wild within it. Have you heard this phrase? Structure sets you free.

BE OPEN TO POSSIBILITY

Creativity comes from putting together two or more things, events, or ideas to create something new. All collaborative decisions are creations. In my view, supporting creativity is critical to making good decisions. The two most common ways that I support group creativity are 1) by using all kinds of tools and techniques for widespread inclusivity and multiple ways of participation, and (2) by establishing clear boundaries within which people feel safe and free. When you are clear about the boundaries and encourage all players in the sandbox, you get creativity. When you make the soil fertile, nature finds a way to grow stuff.

When water mingles with seeds, fertile soil supports the interaction. Germination happens because the soil—the support system—holds the water next to the seed so the water can seep into it. Make your decision-making environment a fertile one. Through the design of your meetings and communications, your ground rules or operating norms, deliberately support the interaction of multiple ideas. Help water and seed connect. Develop a culture of support and nurturing for new ideas.

In group settings, it can work well to separate understanding from creating. We suspend judgment and learn all we can (understanding) before coming to conclusions (creating). Understanding is the basis for all our beliefs and all our actions. Making sure that we all have the same understanding is critical. It helps everyone launch from a level field.

Be aware about crossing the line between understanding the situation (learning) and solving the problem (creating). During group conversations, ask questions before offering advice. In meetings, be sure you fully understand the proposal before giving your opinions about it. Misunderstanding, the source of almost all disagreements between well-intentioned people, tend to disappear when

WHEN EVERYONE CAN SEE ALL THE EVIDENCE, THE RIGHT THING TO DO BECOMES SELF-EVIDENT.

we take the time to understand where others are coming from and how things look from other points of view. Misunderstandings, presumptions, and premature judgments almost always result in bad decisions. Shared understanding is the basis for creative, peaceful, enduring decisions.

Take time to learn the facts, learn each other's perspectives, learn about the possible consequences of specific actions, and learn the depths of each person's feelings on a particular topic. Rarely does an issue get decided upon its first consideration by those aspiring to make good group decisions. This is because we know that differences in understanding lead people to different conclusions and so as a rule, the time spent learning and building shared understanding is usually worth it. When everyone can see all the evidence, the right thing to do becomes self-evident.

If you want to facilitate real collaboration and creativity, be open to all possibilities. If you truly want the best decision for the group as a whole, your evidence-gathering may take a while and might include many conversations, several meetings, and time for individual processing. If there is not enough time, decide only as much as you have good information to support. Guessing, gambling, or rushing to judgment often causes more problems later.

INSIGHT: Write on the Walls

People like to feel heard and when they are, it often allows the group to move forward. A very effective way for someone to feel heard is by writing their point for everyone to see. You can use markers and a flip chart, a laptop and projector, or an online shared screen. People known as graphic facilitators might tape a huge piece of paper to the wall and draw pictures to represent what's being said or agreed, probably with words too, like a comic book.

When someone comments on a topic, you might paraphrase them on a paper chart or on a screen. The words don't need to be perfect—just representative of the view expressed. When the group seems to agree to something, capture it in writing. Make sure everyone understands and accepts the representative words. Writing down words that represent people's viewpoints and agreements is a learned skill and requires focused effort. When done well, it leads to shared understanding and helps people feel empowered.

HOW TO KEEP MOVING FORWARD

When a group gets stuck in the process somewhere, the most important question to ask is not "Why are we stuck?" or "Whose fault is it that we're stuck?" but "How do we move forward?" Getting unstuck often requires an attitude change—a choice to see things differently, to imagine things better, or to decide to let go of something. It also often requires creative thinking about the next steps that could be taken in spite of the situation or attitudes of others. And it requires *doing* something—not just wishing for things to change.

If moving forward is important to you and your group, be creative and take a single step, no matter how small. Don't get bogged down complaining about the situation or trying to figure out why things are the way they are. Rather, accept the situation and say, "Now what do we do?" Find a way. Go around. Make new partners. Try something different.

I was working with the board of directors of a private school who wanted to build a high school adjacent to its existing grade school campus. The school owned some adjacent land, but after some research, the board deemed it impossible to build there due to the cost. They seemed stuck. Yet some people took the initiative to look for a place that the school could rent for a few years while money was raised to build on the adjacent land. The school found a place and ran a high school in a rented building for many years. Even though the board members couldn't have all they wanted, they found a work-around—a next step in the desired direction. An unanticipated benefit: running the high school in a rented space for a few years gave the school valuable experience when it came to design their own. Breaking projects into pieces allows us to learn before taking next steps.

If you're stuck, another solution is to take a straw vote. The best group decisions are based on shared understanding of everyone's perspective, and a good way to get a quick read of where everyone stands is to take a straw vote. A straw vote is not a real vote, and it doesn't count in the long run. Someone might say, "Let's just see how people feel about the latest idea. All those who tend to like it, show a thumbs-up. If you tend not to like it, show a thumbs-down. If you are neutral or undecided, show a sideways thumb." Count the thumbs in the three categories. It lets everyone in the group see, in a quick and general way, if the latest idea is worth more group time and energy. It also shows where the concerns are (the thumbs-down), so we know who to call on to hear concerns. Some groups use color cards for straw votes. Some use on-screen apps. Before calling for a straw vote, make sure the question is clear and simple. You don't want to waste group time haggling about a proposal or decision that is unclear. No matter how they are done, the most efficient groups use straw votes often and with ease.

When calling for a straw vote, remind everyone that we're not making a final decision and that everyone has the right to change their mind later. It's just a quick snapshot of how the group feels at this moment. Still, even a snapshot can be worth a thousand words.

Or you might do a multi-vote—where each group member is given three or more votes to allocate among several alternatives. For instance, after identifying several ways to solve a problem and posting them around the room or in an online survey, each group member might be given five votes (small sticker-dots in person) and told, "Put your sticker-dots on your five favorite ideas." Placing two or even three stickers on a single item is typically allowed. After voting, the whole group can step back and see how the votes are distributed among all the ideas. There is often an immediate shared sense of the group's top priorities. I find that the best use of a multi-vote is to determine where to focus conversation. Rather than continue conversation about a whole list of ideas, multi-vote results indicate which ideas are worth further group consideration and which are not.

I believe that all worthy creations are a combination of art and technique. I learned this from studying Martin Heidegger in college.[31] Most group decision-making processes are all about technique—what **NOTHING BRINGS** to do and in what order—yet why not **TOGETHER A GROUP** add music, stories, and pictures into **LIKE EVERYONE** your group decision-making. I've been **LAUGHING.** in situations where the whole group is asked to make a drawing together or make a skit or a TV ad or a TikTok. You might think it's a little touchy-feely and not right for all groups—and it's never OK to put someone on the spot or out of their comfort zone without their permission—yet visual representation of ideas is not to be underestimated. And nothing brings together a group like everyone laughing. Allow time and space for creative expression and discovery. Processes that encourage risk and creativity can be incredibly valuable, especially when it seems there is no other answer in sight. The process that creates the solution will almost always be different than the process that created the problem.

People often arrive at similar solutions from different paths. For example, deciding how much money to spend on something

---

31 Martin Heidegger, *The Question Concerning Technology and Other Essays* (1997).

is almost always a convergence of what the group wants and what the group can afford. Some people arrive at the number by exploring what they want. Others come at such a number by exploring what they can afford. With big decisions like buying a house, a car, or a factory, we focus for a while on what we can afford, and we home in on a range. Then we focus on what we want (what type of house, car, or factory) and home in on a range for that. We go back and forth and where these two converge is our solution.

11. LOGIC AND FAITH, BOTH REQUIRED

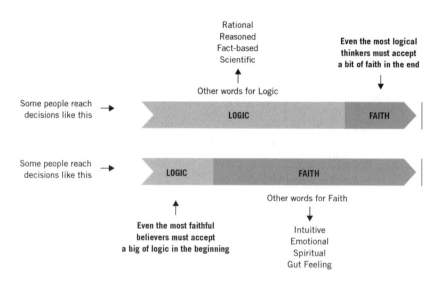

Sometimes a person arrives at a solution mostly by logic and another person arrives at a similar solution mostly by gut feeling. People with rational personalities want as much evidence as possible with a wee bit of trust. Intuitive personalities are happy with just a wee bit of evidence and lots of trust. Sometimes I arrive at a solution by trial and error, sometimes by YouTube learning, sometimes by chatting with friends. Whatever paths are taken—logic, intuition, YouTube, gossip—look for where multiple paths seem to converge on common solutions. Where people get to the same place by two different means, that's worth more exploration.

INSIGHT: For Real Results: Focus

If you want to maximize your collaborative effectiveness, resist the temptation to check other screens, have side conversations, or work on other projects during the meeting. Even if you are bored or think you have nothing to contribute, stay focused and search within for creative solutions. Listen to others in attendance in order to develop a deeper understanding or quietly jot down notes on how things could be better. Discourage other group members from weaving in and out of participation. Some people even try prayer and meditation during a meeting, believing that the magic of groups happens when several brains and hearts are focused on a single task, even if silent.

Multitasking is increasingly popular, but the fact remains that focusing on one goal at a time is the best way to achieve your top goals. Groups are especially prone to failure when trying to do too many things at once, and especially prone to success when everyone is focused on a single task.

SOMETIMES AN IDEA SHOULD DIE

A community club has a yard sale every year on the Saturday of Memorial Day weekend. They have always had a yard sale on the Saturday of Memorial Day weekend. The task of setting up and taking down the yard sale is a huge amount of work, there are fewer volunteers every year, and the sale is making less and less money each year. So why does the club keep doing it?

It's crucial for groups to regularly evaluate their activities in light of what each activity is supposed to achieve. Such an evaluation—even if done quickly as part of the annual budgeting process—helps groups analyze whether commitments to specific issues are growing or waning. It helps groups make choices about what to continue and what to drop. Spending precious energy on activities that don't add value or attract energy hampers efficiency and distracts attention from value-adding activities.

Let's say someone has an idea. Someone may suggest forming a committee to explore the idea. "Anyone want to serve on this committee?" the facilitator asks. No hands go up. At such a moment, it is surprising how many groups will form a committee anyway, perhaps "volunteer" others to be on it, and feel they have successfully dealt with the issue. Don't do this. If there is no energy for something, let it die. If no one present wants to be on the committee, don't form the committee.

One way to respect the dying process is to plan for it. When you launch a committee or project, build in a sunset provision that says the thing will die on a certain date (perhaps months or years into the future) if the group doesn't vote to extend it. To keep it alive, someone has to act. That way, when it dies, it is nobody's fault and was expected all along.

The wonderful thing about death is that it always leads to

new things. New understandings, new leadership, new relationships. To me the first principle of all energy is that it never goes away, it goes into other things. When things die, the energy goes to other places. Good energy always finds its way to new, creative uses.

INSIGHT: Quitting Is Underrated

In spite of the "succeed at all costs" ethic that surrounds us, sometimes quitting is the right decision. Of course, we know that persistence leads to success and that success often requires "hanging in there." But persistence and "hanging in there" can also lead to losing money, losing health, and losing friends. Walking away is often the most practical thing to do, especially when it's thoughtful, deliberate, and strategic.

When groups do strategic planning, they are often quick to add programs, products, and services that can result in unrealistic or unsustainable strategic plans. But for strategic planning to result in realistic and sustainable plans, put equal thought into what to cut.

Don't quit something on a whim or in anger or in haste, but if letting go or getting out really is the best strategy to achieve a higher objective, do it. Unfounded fear of cutting a program or severing a relationship can paralyze a group and cause huge expenses over time. Quit while you are ahead.

PART IV

EVEN WHEN WE DISAGREE

CHAPTER 15

It Matters How We Listen

WE CAN GET along with each other and be productive together even when we disagree with each other. We don't need to let conflict paralyze us or divide us. There seems to be a rising myth in America that it's OK to discount, ignore, and otherwise be mean to people who disagree with us. For me this is a great sadness, and I think it's untrue. It doesn't have to be this way. There's no need.

I choose to believe that we actually don't have to agree in order to get along and do great things together. I rather like the notion of welcoming disagreement and working through it. Let's work side by side anyway, even though we see things differently. To me the mark of a great leader is not that they can defeat their enemies, but that they can get along with their enemies.

If I want to get along with someone, step one is to listen to what they have to say. Good communication—listening and talking, reading and writing—is critical for understanding. Understanding is the basis for all of our beliefs and actions—critical for good group decisions—and listening is the pipeline that fuels understanding.

ALL VIEWS ARE VALID

In hierarchical relationships, the person at the top has a wider view than the people below. If you have ever climbed a mountain or tall building, you know that you see more the higher you are. The supervisor considers the opinions of their subordinate, but many other things also. Similarly, the elected representative and the constituent have different views, at different scales. The constituent has one problem in a specific part of the district, yet the elected representative needs to consider a huge variety of interests across the district and also has pressure from their party and other places too. This type of tension—making people work together who see things differently by the nature of their role—is built into all the operations of institutions. It keeps us accountable, and it pushes us to be creative.

Deliberately seeking out and then putting together different views from different places and at different scales is extremely valuable in a number of ways. Here's how you do it. Step one is to build it into the culture and practices of the organization. If you are a company, establish cross-disciplinary or cross-occupational teams to do creative tasks. Emphasize peer-to-peer learning and mutual support. Require that accommodations are made not only to include but to encourage all voices in providing feedback, planning, and decision-making. Provide training on how to collaborate, how to be a good team, how to be inclusive. Reward and publicly praise people who are demonstrating inclusion and collaboration.

If you are a government entity making public policy, deliberately seek out and encourage people and perspectives not traditionally heard. Do this not for the purpose of meeting a legal requirement but because it will result in better public policy! In fact, good public policy development *requires* that we hear about the full range of concerns, about all the ideas for solutions, and all the possible consequences of various approaches. Deliberately seek them out and get them to the table.

Ask people to say how things are for them and how things look from where they sit. And listen to what they say. Ask them in ways that they will understand what you are asking and ask questions that they will be comfortable answering. This is critical in cross-cultural or emotionally charged situations. Show respect. Ask baby-step questions. Ask outsiders, "What does it look like from out there?" Listen without judgment. If you are asked to give your view, offer it without expectation that it will prevail. Speak for yourself, from your own perspective. Humbly offer a piece of the puzzle to help create the larger picture.

Share stories. This is the time-honored way of conflict resolution. Listen to the stories of others without interruption, wanting to learn "how it was for them." And share stories from your own point of view. When I am asked to mediate an existing conflict between two parties, there is a time early on in the process where I ask them to simply tell and hear each other's stories without interruption. That's all. Tell stories. Ask questions. No conclusions or actions steps. End of session. When we take the time to tell one another where we're coming from, stuff after that becomes easier.

The best way to start sharing stories is to ask questions. Even though you might have your own opinion forming in your head, hold off expressing your opinion and start with questions instead. Be genuinely open to changing your opinion based on new things you learn. Good questions are open-ended and start with *why*, *how*, and *what*, such as "Why do you think that? How has it worked well in the past? What do you think is the cause of the problem?"

When I begin a discussion with a question, I show respect for others and indicate that I want to hear what they have to say. Most conflicts are due to misunderstanding, so when my opinion is based on presumption, I'm probably headed for conflict. The longer I remain open-minded, the greater the chances that my opinion is based on a more complete understanding. When we start conversations with questions, we're less threatening to others, we're more likely to develop a well-informed opinion, and we're helping the group avoid conflict.

Demonstrate Listening

Messages often get changed between how they are launched and how they land. The person talking often means one thing yet the person listening often hears it differently due to differences in culture, context, and perspective. Actually, this almost always happens. Count on it. And it's nobody's fault. Yet the more you hear things incorrectly or not at all, the more likely you are to proceed on false assumptions that are likely to collapse later and cause conflict. The best way to ensure good listening is to demonstrate it. How do you do that? You prove it.

When someone speaks to you, demonstrate that you are listening and that you understand what is being said. Saying "I understand" is not a demonstration. First of all, as you listen, show that you are paying attention with silent expressions or eye contact and perhaps an encouraging nod or two at the right times. Further, use your own words to describe what you just heard and how the words landed on you. This allows the speaker to clarify any difference between launch and land. And if you missed, no problem. Keep going back and forth until you get it right. This is how we advance and demonstrate understanding.

Want to demonstrate even more? Actually do things based on what the person said. Change your behavior. Make sure they notice.

OUT OF SILENCE, ANYTHING CAN HAPPEN

Silence in groups is largely underrated and often misunderstood. We've all been in situations when silence befalls the group for only a moment and someone says, "I can't stand the silence," and then they launch into talking about something that may or may not be useful. Such a person would rather empty their head on us than endure a single moment of silence. And many people are like that.

Many of us are raised with the belief that silence indicates inactivity or a lack of productivity. Some people can't cope with the appearance that the group is doing nothing. Others are uncomfortable with group silence because they fear the unknown. Silence may suggest lack of structure, doubt about what is going to happen next, who is in charge, or vulnerability.

But here's the thing: Out of silence anything can happen. I love libraries because of their silence—nature walks too. Situations where there is no plan for what might fill the air. When we are making group decisions, silence makes room for important activity. Silence clears the air of clutter so vital things can show up. Silence is an opening of all channels. Silence is fertile ground for creativity. In a conflict with someone? Get yourself in their presence and be silent. Just go along. See what comes.

We cannot expect to learn new things from other people or from our inner selves if we are blabbering away about things we already know. When we listen in silence with intent to understand, we are doing much more than letting information flow in. We are processing that information and attempting to draw conclusions. Not only does silence allow us to fully hear others and understand them, it also gives us space to hear our own thoughts and feelings. When we are silent, we are evaluating the credibility of what we hear. We are weighing it against other things we have heard. We are organizing the information in ways easier for us to grasp. We are recognizing nuances of tone and inflection and considering how these affect the meaning. We are imagining what it is like to feel what the speaker feels. We are imagining how others are reacting. We are trying to make sense of what we are hearing. We are trying to do more than just hear. We are trying to understand.

Many groups practice a brief moment of silence between each speaker. Some groups, like my Quaker Meeting, for example, practice long periods of silence in between speakers. While not common in most meetings, brief periods of silence in between speakers and longer periods of silence here and there throughout a meeting give people a chance to process the information that has been coming in. When a meeting to learn about a topic is scheduled separately from a meeting to make decisions about the topic, members have a chance to process the information between meetings so that it can lead to understanding. An unfortunate fact is that it is possible to have an abundance of information and no understanding. Information without understanding is just information. Silence makes room for discernment—the translation of information into understanding.

It's rarely helpful to speak up with the first thing that comes to mind. Even when there's a sense of urgency—in fact, *especially* when there's a sense of urgency—we are better off if we take time to breathe, reflect, and consider our words before speaking them. I once heard someone say, "I thank God for the split second I have learned to place between my thoughts and my words." Those split seconds can save hours of anxiety and avoid unnecessary tension and potentially huge inefficiencies in the group. If tensions in a group are high, call for a break or a few moments of silence before proceeding.

There is often a presumption that those who speak first know most. This is far from true. Just because a person is talking doesn't necessarily mean they are contributing or that they're the only one contributing. Much of the time in a group decision setting, listening is the best contribution a person can make. It is through listening, not talking, that we develop understanding, compassion, and creative solutions.

One of the simplest but most important decisions you have to make every moment you're in a group is whether you're going to open your mouth or keep it shut. Whether you're going to talk or listen. My experience tells me it works well to set the default switch to *listen* and speak up only if—

- You personally care about the issue and have a real stake in it.

- You understand the issue enough to add useful, accurate information.

- No one else has already said it, even with different words.

- There's been an invitation, and it's the right time for speaking on the issue.

If *each* of these four conditions are met *or* if you have strong feelings that are screaming to be shared then—yes!—please speak up. Others will benefit from your words. Otherwise, it's best to listen.

INSIGHT: Benefits When You Let Someone Else Talk First

If you let another person talk while you listen, it gives you some practical advantages:

- Hearing where they are coming from helps you choose your words. They have likely provided you with some new information that you can incorporate into your style or actual words back to them.

- Once they have gotten their words out, they are more likely to be open to hearing yours.

- Not talking gives you time to listen to your own thoughts and feelings. While they are talking, you're not just listening to them, you're listening to you.

ADVICE IS BEST WHEN
REQUESTED AND UNCONDITIONAL

If you give advice only when asked, you are on solid ground and it will minimize your chances for regrets. If your advice has strings, conditions, or expectations, that's a setup for your own disappointment. Besides, requested advice without strings is much more useful to the receiver. Better decisions are made when the decider is free to act on all, part of, or none of the advice you have given. In my opinion, unsolicited advice is called for only when an intervention is truly warranted. By this I mean doing something against someone's will "for their own good."

It works well to ask for advice with specifics and parameters. You might ask for comments on a written proposal or answers to a specific question. Or you might describe a specific situation and ask, "What would you do?"

If you're on the receiving end of advice that you have asked for, accept it with appreciation whether you like it or not. You can praise the messenger even if you hate the message. If you are on the receiving end of unsolicited advice, and if you are grown-ups on a level playing field, you are under no obligation to take it. You are the boss of you.

FEEDBACK PLEASE. HEAR! HEAR!

Where advice is about what to do going forward, feedback is about what happened in the past. Whenever we are trying to achieve results in a group setting, it always helps to ask for feedback. When we do, we increase our chances of getting optimum results. Asking for feedback takes courage, but it helps us see things in new light reflected off of others. If we don't ask, we can't fully expect people to tell us what's going well and what isn't. And when we do ask, we should be open to any and all answers.

When requesting feedback, ask what could be better. Find out what questions or ideas your stakeholders have. Be open to how you might use the feedback to make improvements, whether the feedback is positive or negative. Take positive comments to heart and share credit with others. When you receive a negative comment, consider that it's probably not about you. It's more likely about a particular idea, behavior, or situation that you are associated with. Often, negative comments are all about the private world of the commentator and have nothing to do with the topic at hand or the person named. The feedback opportunity becomes a vehicle for someone to act out; someone who is angry or bored. If you ask for feedback, you should at least look at what people say and decide on a comment-by-comment basis what requires corrective action and what can be legitimately ignored.

A quick way to do feedback: When someone says something you agree with, show your approval instantly with a "hear, hear" or a head nod or a thumbs-up. It is useful for the whole group to see such cues. Accentuated cues are especially useful in online meetings where our views of each other might be small. Other variations include keypad voting and standing line-ups (in an in-person meeting, I ask everyone to stand and line up from one end of the room to the other to let everyone see where each person stands on a particular issue). If your general view is expressed by someone else, restrain your need to present the view in a different way with a different spin with a few extra tidbits of information. Quakers are known to say: "That Friend speaks my mind."

INSIGHT: Direct Is Best

The shortest distance between two points is a direct straight line. When it comes to communications between two people, the shorter the better. Yet it's often way easier to get information indirectly, and usually way more fun. You might even call it gossip. Indirect information can be very entertaining.

If you are wondering what someone thinks about something, or why they did something, or what they plan to do in the future, ask them directly. Get the story straight from the source. If you want someone to know what you think, or why you did something, or what you plan to do, tell them. Don't be silent, sneaky, or circuitous or "let them figure it out." When you hear information indirectly like "she thinks this" or "he said that," know that what you are hearing is out of context, altered by the messenger, and only one side of the story.

HAVING THE HARD CONVERSATIONS

Sometimes the barrier to direct communication is a mechanical nature, such as language or physical proximity or simply a lack of direct personal or professional connection. Sometimes it's cultural. There are many natural barriers. Yet we need to push through such barriers, at least try. Better to reach out to someone of a different culture awkwardly than not at all. Better to bumble and maybe say the wrong thing than to make no effort at all. At least make an effort. If nothing else, through your sheer humility and vulnerability you can demonstrate your intentions to get along.

Often the biggest barrier to having a conversation is our

fear. We don't trust ourselves to say the right things or react the right ways. We are afraid that in a one-on-one setting we will lose the battle we are trying to win. We are afraid of getting hurt. So for all these legitimate reasons we might avoid the situation or person, assume a position of superiority, or try to come up with new rules or procedures to avoid the issue. But none of these actions are likely to make the tension go away over the long run.

INSIGHT: Focus on Curiosity

Just after President Donald Trump was elected, I organized a series of conversations between Republicans and Democrats in Maine. The forums—open to all types of people with all political views—were called Make Shift Coffee Houses, and the effort won the American Award for Civic Collaboration in 2019.

At the start of almost every conversation, I told the people: "You are allowed to be curious about someone else's beliefs without changing your own." I have seen this sentence bring audible expressions of relief or aha. This attitude is disarming. When I see the upcoming conversation not as a competition but as a learning opportunity, it makes it easier. "Maybe I'll just check it out," I might say to myself. "Maybe I'll just ask some questions and learn some stuff." That's a pretty good attitude.

Another thing that we sometimes said at the start of a Make Shift Coffee House: "You are allowed to walk out of this room with exactly the same beliefs you walked in here with." When I know that from the start, it makes it easier for me to enter the room.

How you see conflict and tension in general—your attitude toward it—matters. It works well to not view tensions as battles to be won or lost but rather as shared problems to be solved in shared ways. So before doing anything else, seek first to find a way to talk with those who are involved in the tension. If there are mechanical barriers to talking, work to fix them. If there are personal emotional barriers in the way, work to fix them. Take a look at your own attitudes and behaviors. If you are part of the problem, have a talk with yourself.

I might want to have a specific conversation with someone but it would be too awkward to just bring it up. Asking for a phone call or a meeting would make it too big of a deal. Talking about it would likely help the tension between us, but trying to force a conversation could make matters worse. In such a situation you might look for ways to interact with the person unrelated to the issue at hand. Get yourself situated to do something

TAKE A LOOK AT YOUR OWN ATTITUDES AND BEHAVIORS. IF YOU ARE PART OF THE PROBLEM, HAVE A TALK WITH YOURSELF.

with the person, perhaps working on the same team or project. Do stuff side by side. If you are holding a specific intention for a specific conversation with someone, and you spend enough time with them, you will easily find the right time to raise your issue. Be patient. Invest. It will come up when the time is right. It won't feel awkward. It will help you both.

And if someone else proposes a way to talk with you about a shared problem, accept the opportunity. Always talk. Find a way.

Resist the Temptation to Speak for Others

Speak for yourself and encourage others to speak for themselves. Help create a group culture of support and respect so that people are not shy about speaking and standing up for themselves. When information is delivered on behalf of others, take it at half value.

There are times when speaking on behalf of someone else or on behalf of a class of people is appropriate, and in fact called for. There are times when a group should rightfully consider voices not present. Yet if we are trying to develop shared understanding and a person isn't in the room to answer our questions, we should not proceed based on "what we think they might say" if we can help it.

The best way to incorporate perspectives of marginalized people into your conversations is not to arrange for someone to try and speak for them but to bring them to the table and encourage them to speak for themselves. It takes effort. It might require bridging cultural divides. Yet it's not only highly effective, it's highly efficient to engage the right people with key perspectives right from the start. It prevents conflict and unintended consequences later. And once in the room, everyone can speak for themselves. Such a group can often make very good decisions very quickly. It's amazing how much you can get done quickly with the perfect assembly of people in the room.

A NOTE ABOUT THE INTERNET: WE'RE LEARNING

The internet has had a major impact on how we communicate with each other, how we listen to each other, and where we get our information. No doubt about it, new internet technologies hold a lot of promise for group decision-making. The Internet allows us to convey and receive information with efficiency like never before. It allows many more of us to have access to good information. It allows us to organize and mobilize like never before. It allows us to collaborate remotely like never before. Yet it also brings significant concerns and threats to good group decision-making.

Since humans first evolved about 2,500,000 years ago, we have been smiling, frowning, frolicking, and fighting with each other. We have always made group decisions with facial expressions and body movements, and as a result we are really, really good at receiving and conveying information that way. Between 30,000 and 70,000 years ago, we developed verbal language skills. We've been practicing those for a really long time too.

Now, though, we are in the dawn of a new way of communicating with each other. We've only been communicating via the internet for the past thirty years, for just 0.0012 percent of our time on earth. And honestly, we are really bad at it. And at this stage of evolution, I'm not ready to bless one technology, software, or approach over another. Whatever I might say on paper is sure to be obsolete soon anyway. Things are changing fast at the dawn of this new era. And besides, the fundamentals of human nature—of collaboration—are at play no matter what software you are running. We're still humans. We feel glad, sad, mad, and scared just as we always have.[32] We struggle to balance ego and humility, self-interest with group interests, greed with compassion, just as we have for thousands of generations.

---

32 These are widely considered to be the four basic human emotions. [This for citation if needed: https://www.theatlantic.com/health/archive/2014/02/new-research-says-there-are-only-four-emotions/283560/]

DIGITAL MEDIA: LIKE A CHAINSAW

Direct messages (DMs), email messages, text messages, and social media comments are highly effective ways to communicate in groups. They are instant like talking, enduring like a written document, and able to be copied and distributed like nothing we have ever known. This new way of communicating is revolutionary. And highly effective. Yet the combination of these three things makes digital media rather like a chainsaw: effective when used properly and dangerous when used on impulse or in anger. DMs, email, text messages, and social media comments are most effective when they're used to convey facts quickly. They are most destructive when used to convey negative reactions and/or intentional deceit.

Sending or posting digital comments is so quick and easy that we are apt to forget that what we write may be distributed far and wide and long after the feelings behind the message have subsided. And very few of us are skilled enough to convey exactly what we mean with written words or to discern exactly what the words we receive were meant to convey. Digital messages are easily misunderstood, and as we know, misunderstanding is usually at the root of bad decisions and the resulting conflict.

Beware of using digital media to convey negative emotions, arguments, or sarcasm. It's easy to use these platforms to say something hurtful about someone, but not to their face, yet in front to thousands.

If you don't have something nice to say, don't say it by DM, email, text message, or in a social media comment. If you don't fully understand something that someone sent you or posted, try not to fill in the blanks with assumptions. If you don't understand what the sender meant, ask them if you can. The moment someone indicates that they just want to provoke conflict or drama, drop them.

INTERNET CHALLENGES FOR GOOD GROUP DECISIONS

The internet allows us to intentionally deceive each other like never before. For one thing, it lets us be anonymous. And cowardly. Fake personas and fake news stand blatantly in the way of good group decisions and work aggressively against shared understanding, collaboration, and moving toward peace. These tools are created to serve specific interests via the use of intentional deception and manipulation. But these tools are being used within our country against fellow citizens and in all sorts of communities against each other.

INSIGHT: Zero Tolerance for Fake Personas

Dishonesty and closed-mindedness have no place in good group decisions. If you have people who are intentionally trying to deceive others in the group (such as with fake personas and fake news), you will simply not be able to make good group decisions. And if you have people in your group who are not open to new information and new ways of looking at things, you will fail at making good group decisions.

And another ominous challenge: news feed algorithms. A machine decides what information you get based on what information it thinks you want. Of course, newspapers have done this for years. They print the news they think their customers might most likely want to read. That's how they sell papers. But in the case of the *New York Times* or any other national newspaper, everyone in the country—liberals, conservatives, artists, engineers—gets almost the same paper. In the case of news via social media such as Facebook, Twitter, or Instagram, however, we're all getting very different news.

More and more of us are getting more and more of our news from social media sources, according to a recent report by the Pew Research Center. More than half of US adults get news from social media *often* or *sometimes*.[33] This is a huge concern because while most Americans get their news from social media, most Americans feel that news on social media is biased or inaccurate.

---

33 Elisa Shearer and Elizabeth Grieco, "Americans Are Wary of the Roles Social Media Sites Play in Delivering the News," Pew Research Center, October 2, 2019.

CHAPTER 16

Ways to Get Along

CONFLICT IS A part of life. Tension is critical for all systems. Ideas grow through conflict. Character grows through conflict. Organizations and communities evolve through conflict. Most of us don't like conflict when it's happening or when we think it's going to happen, yet handling conflict is part of being human. The trick is to navigate and manage conflict in ways that are helpful rather than harmful over the long run. In spite of conflict, there are ways to get along and be productive and be happy.

Like health care is in the realm of disease prevention, management, and cure, peacemaking is in the realm of conflict prevention, management, and resolution. An ounce of prevention is worth a pound of cure; that's how the popular saying goes. It's true with health care and it's true with peacemaking: Investing in prevention gives you your best bang for the buck. That's where you want to put your effort to maximize group efficiency. Whether you're a married couple, members of a council, or nations at the negotiating table, putting effort into preventing conflict tends to be a wise expenditure of time and money in terms of cost and benefits.

Talk first before taking action. Talk a lot. Talk to lots of people. As a rule, talking is conflict prevention. I sometimes wonder why, instead of sending highly equipped and trained soldiers to a troubled region of the world, we don't send highly equipped and trained talkers. I often wish we could be patient and invest in huge, widespread, well-organized conversations before pulling any triggers.

Also like with health care, once you are in a conflict, it's helpful to diagnose the problem and know what stage you're at. Knowing the nature of the problem helps you identify the right resolution. If you feel a cold coming on, you take some Vitamin C. If you feel a conflict "coming on," you do a personal inventory and consider your part—what you did to contribute to the conflict and what you can do to make peace.

TWO PATHS TO PEACE

If I'm in conflict internally or with others in my group, I have basically two paths to peace: I can do something about it or I can let go of it. I can either work to change things for the better or I can work to accept things as they are. When I feel conflict, I mentally draw a circle around the things that I can actually do something about, the things I can change. I define the circle of things within my control and work to change them. I let go of everything outside the circle. I might not like what's happening "out there"—outside my control—but I choose to make peace with it because I can't do anything about it anyway. In other words, define your part, take responsibility for improving your part, and do not

12. WHAT TO CHANGE AND ACCEPT

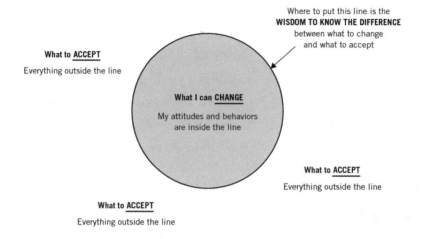

take on other parts. When you work inside the circle—addressing the things you can change—it's all about action. It's about *doing* things differently. When you work outside the circle, it's all about acceptance. It's about *seeing* things differently.

Now here's the tricky part: Where do you draw the line—the boundary between what to accept and what to change? It's what the Serenity Prayer calls "the wisdom to know the difference."[34]

Let's say I'm a member of the city council, and I have proposed a dog park on the south side of town three times in a row. And my proposal has gotten shot down three times in a row. This is causing huge conflict for me. One of the reasons I ran for city council was to push this dog park and it's going nowhere. OK. Breathe. What are my choices? If I think that this is a fight I want to fight, then I need to come up with some new strategies to win. I could work with my fellow councilors one on one. I could mobilize supporters.

---

34 The Serenity Prayer is thought to have been written by Reinhold Niebuhr. Here are the famous first three lines: "God grant me the courage to change the things I can, the serenity to accept the things I can't, and the wisdom to know the difference."

I could ramp up my antagonism at city council meetings. Yet I could also choose to let go of the dog park issue for now. Really let go. Fully accept that I misread the council and recognize that a dog park on the south side of town isn't going to happen. So I turn my attention to other things. I move on.

Sometimes working outside the circle and accepting things might seem like giving up. And you know what? Sometimes that's exactly what it is. And you know what? Sometimes that's exactly what's needed. We have all heard many versions of "Don't ever give up." Sounds good, and easy to go along with, but often that is terrible advice and the cause of many a conflict. Often, walking away is absolutely the best solution.

MAKING PEACE IS ALWAYS AN INSIDE JOB.

Acceptance is often the most viable path to inner peace. Surrender is not always a bad thing. It's way underrated. If you really want to make peace with a situation, your answer might be to accept it rather than change it, surrender to it rather than fight it. Acceptance can be really hard, yet it can tame conflict.

At times you will not be able to accept things as they are, nor should you. If you are oppressed or working for those oppressed, you may find you need to change the things you can. You might need to fight. Sometimes it's fighting that brings me peace; it allows me to live with myself because I'm doing what I can.

In any event, I have found that making peace is always an inside job. It has everything to do with the choices we make about where to draw that line and how we act inside it. I once attended a conflict management class where I thought I was going to learn how to manage difficult people. Turns out I learned that conflict management is all about managing myself.

INSIGHT: Letting Go Is a Choice

There's the story of two monks who walked together in silence for days. They came upon a shallow river and saw a young woman on the banks wanting to cross but needing help. The monks were sworn to help anyone in distress, yet also sworn to never touch a woman. One of the monks made a swift decision, picked up the woman, and carried her across the river. He put her down on the other side, and the two monks walked on in silence, with the other monk fretting. He couldn't believe what he had just seen. His comrade had done something so wrong! He carried his turmoil silently for days. When he could stand it no more, he stopped on the path and exclaimed, "How could you carry her across the river!" The first monk replied, "I carried her across the river, but put her down on the other side."

SHARE EXPECTATIONS TO MINIMIZE CONFLICT

Disagreements usually stem from mismatched expectations. Where the expectations are vastly different, and/or the stakes are very high, the conflict can be huge. When two or more people have a shared task, they do well to figure out their shared expectations and note them in writing or say them verbally so they can solidify that shared understanding. Contracts are shared expectations written down with formality—as are ground rules, guidelines, and bylaws. The creation of these written documents forces us to put our expectations clearly in the open for all parties to see. When you don't take time to clarify expectations with those you later plan to depend on, you will find yourself disappointed.

People in disagreement with each other often stop disagreeing precisely at the point one of them says, "Oh, I didn't realize that . . . " or "Well, if I had known . . . " Most disagreements are due to a lack of understanding rather than a genuine clash of values, and are easily solved by having quality conversations. Taking the time to talk may seem like a waste of time, but conversations can ignite understanding in ways that no other technique can.

To prevent misunderstandings, get the story straight from the source, hear all perspectives, listen to understand, be open-minded, and don't be afraid to change your mind. That includes with people you may consider enemies. Before deciding or doing anything, invite your enemies to talk about the issue so you can seek to understand their perspectives. Look for misunderstandings and clear them up by exchanging information. You might find that you were mistaken in thinking that a particular person or some group was an actual enemy.

If your enemy does not come to the table in good faith but rather sees the table as just another field of battle or intends to use that conversation against you later, that's a problem. It's usually not worth my time to be in a conversation at a table with someone who I suspect is trying to play me. I only want to sit with and make deals with people I can trust.

Sometimes when we talk with our adversaries, we can agree to a resolution that maintains mutual respect and preserves the peace. Sometimes we leave the table with things unresolved. Yet when we genuinely invite our adversaries to problem-solve with us, whether they take up the invitation or not, whether the problem gets solved or not, we are on better footing for going forward.

Try to enter every discussion as if it were a new discussion—with a positive outlook and an open mind about your fellow decision makers—regardless of past or other present disagreements. Don't hold grudges, seek revenge, or use a person's stance on one issue as a weapon against them on another issue. When we are willing to work with open minds and positive attitudes, even with our adversaries, we are most likely to help our group.

BE RESPECTFUL OF EACH OTHER

Some conflicts are more than misunderstandings, they are due to differing core values, which I define as values so deeply held by a person that they are unlikely to be changed by argument or even facts. The key to preventing, managing, and resolving this type of conflict is to take stock of what you do believe in common and tolerate the rest. For example, there are two friends: a Yankees fan and a Red Sox fan. They both love baseball, and they are each OK that the other guy loves a different team. When you show respect for each other's values, you can build something together that you can both agree on, in spite of the stuff you disagree about. Respectfully agree to disagree. Be nice. Don't let your disagreement about one issue prevent you from working together on other issues.

If you do have an adverse reaction to someone's words or actions, stop yourself from reacting right away. Try first to understand the words or behavior you've just

DON'T LET YOUR DISAGREEMENT ABOUT ONE ISSUE PREVENT YOU FROM WORKING TOGETHER ON OTHER ISSUES.

witnessed. Then think carefully about the reaction you want to have and what purpose it will serve. If after a pause you decide that you need to react, even with fury if compelled, do it. You are allowed to say what you need to say to protect yourself. Speaking for yourself about yourself will work best. Or perhaps after a pause you decide to yourself to address the matter later; perhaps talk privately with the person you have an issue with. You might start by asking a question about what they said or did. If you think your group needs to resolve the issue in public, then speak up. Otherwise consider how to manage your adverse reaction in other ways.

And don't let another person's bad behavior serve as an excuse for your own bad behavior. "Well, they're not doing their part so I'm not doing mine." Even if you say this with sophisticated grown-up words, it's still a childish notion. I once heard a family therapist say: "Even just one person working on the relationship will make the relationship better."[35]

And another thing, people have a right to be wrong. Often it is only by being wrong for a while—trying on an idea or approach that doesn't fit—that we come to realize what is right. Without the freedom to be wrong, we often can't get to working on what's right.

If I think you're wrong and I'm right, the question I should ask is not "How can I make you change?" but rather, "Given our different opinions, how shall we move forward together?" For one thing, we agree not to talk down to each other or think bad of each other overall. We agree to work together with respect.

---

35 Paul Charbonneau at the Maine Development Foundation
    Annual Conference, Newry, Maine, 2000.

INSIGHT: Contain Disagreement

Often when there is a disagreement in a group, it's between just two or three people. Or sometimes the main points of the disagreement are represented by just a few of the most outspoken people. While there's a tendency for the whole group to be involved in resolving every disagreement, it need not be that way. If just a few people from your group could come to a resolution, would everyone else go along? If so, who are those people? Get *them* (only them, maybe with a neutral facilitator) working on a resolution and everyone else busy doing other stuff. No need to involve any more people in the conflict than necessary. That's how groups resolve tensions and solve disagreements most efficiently.

ADDRESSING OUTSIDE ISSUES

Some conflicts between people are due to a problem that has nothing to do with the issue at hand. Some incident may have happened to one or both of the parties years ago and has never been dealt with. Someone may have a mental disorder such as an addiction that is warping their judgment or behavior. Perhaps there's a simple misconception closely held since childhood, or an unreasonable fear. Perhaps someone is holding invisible biases or prejudices that are inhibiting your progress.

OUTSIDE ISSUES NEED TO BE FIXED OUTSIDE THE GROUP.

Outside issues are usually personal and often completely unrelated to the group's immediate business. When you see it, name it, perhaps to just one person or perhaps to a group. If it's in the way, it needs to be called out. Recognize that something going on outside the group is unable to be solved by the group. Encourage the parties in conflict to deal with it outside the group. That's the thing about outside issues. They germinated outside the group and so they typically need to be fixed outside the group. Repeat: Outside issues need to be fixed outside the group. I'm talking about therapy, prayer, meditation, support groups, twelve-step work, etc. When people take initiative to work on their own issues outside the group, it can help the group enormously.

OFFER INTERESTS RATHER THAN TAKE POSITIONS

When someone comes into a meeting or a negotiation with an already established position, it limits prospects for creative, innovative, and win-win solutions. When I state my position on an issue early in the discussion, I'm focused thereafter on defending my position and trying to persuade others to agree with it. I might even get sidetracked into defending my pride rather than considering what's best for the group.

On the other hand, if I'm able to speak clearly about my interests (what I would like to get out of the issue without attachment to a particular way of getting it) and I'm able to listen openly to others' interests, the group has a much better chance of getting what it wants.

Focus first on what you really want rather than how to get it. Peel back a layer, dig a bit deeper, and ask, "What desire in me does this solution satisfy or what is my fundamental interest here?" Identify what you are really interested in, give it words, and speak the words to others. Listen carefully to others as they describe their interests. As a group, hear and understand all interests before crafting solutions. Positions spoken early invite argument. Interests spoken clearly invite creative solutions.

It's a well-known negotiation strategy to intentionally with-hold your interests (not say what you really want) to give yourself a competitive edge. If you are in a competition and trying to beat your fellow group member, such deception might be a good short-term strategy. But I believe we have a better chance of actu-ally achieving both of our interests over the long run if we say what they are. You say your interests. I say my interests. Let's work on them together.

CHANGE THE LAW LAST

When someone is upset by a specific situation, they might seek a law-changing remedy. When I see someone drive or park a certain way I might say, "There ought to be a law against that!" I want the police and courts to handle the problem. Similarly, when some-one's behavior at work bothers me, I might ask the boss or the group to make a policy that will regulate that bothersome behavior.

When we ask a larger group to deal with problems more appropriately dealt with on a small scale, huge inefficiencies and later conflicts are likely to result. For starters, any policy change requires a new group decision that takes effort, maybe a lot of effort. Second, small problems often resolve on their own thus rendering arcane some law or policy that might present new problems later. Third, in situations like this the problem is often misrepresented because no one has the courage to be specific.

Therefore, the solution is not perfectly targeted and will likely cause more problems.

Of all the things we can do to solve a problem, seeking a change in law or policy should be the last resort, not the first. The first step is to define the problem honestly, and that means looking at yourself and your contributions. Perhaps you will find that the problem can be solved with a change in your own attitude or behavior. The second step is to reach out and see if the problem might be resolved between just one or two other people. You might ask yourself, *What if I talked privately with* _____? *Could that help solve the problem?* The "fill in the blank" might be your adversary. Step two takes courage. Only after completing steps one and two, or only if the problem repeatedly affects the group as a whole, does it require a group remedy.

A person making their own life better at the expense of public resources is the leading cause of government inefficiency. Public policy is a large blunt instrument designed to handle large problems with blunt force. Using public policy to fix a problem between neighbors can be like using an axe to remove a splinter. Yes, you might remove the splinter, but at what cost? Sometimes a policy or law needs to change. I'm all about making laws better. I'm just reminding us that changing a law or a group policy is rarely the best way to fix a problem.

ALLOW FOR MULTIPLE TRUTHS

Two or more people rarely agree that a certain thing happened exactly the same way or for exactly the same reasons. How things look always depends on where you sit. Two people can see the same thing differently. In other words, there can be multiple truths. Does this mean that one is right and one is wrong, or that one is lying and one is telling the truth? Maybe, but if they are honest people with good intentions, they are probably both telling the truth as they see it.

Groups can spend huge amounts of energy and create huge amounts of conflict trying to agree on a single version of the truth. Often, it doesn't matter to the whole group what really happened or why, and our group will be much better served if we can find a solution that honors all truths—whatever they are. Instead of insisting on "this *or* that," try "this *and* that." Allow that seemingly contradictory things can be true

THE BEST GROUP DECISIONS ARE ALWAYS CREATED FROM MULTIPLE TRUTHS.

simultaneously for different people with different perspectives. It's amazing how much conflict can be avoided, how much respect can be preserved, and how much creativity can unfold when we allow for multiple truths. In fact, the best group decisions are always created from multiple truths.

CONCLUSION

BENEFITS OF BELONGING

My friend Melissa was an addict. She was addicted to alcohol, marijuana, sex, heroin, and other things. She was a loner, only caring about the next high. Her "friends" were really just vehicles for getting the next high. Much of her life she was unhappy, angry, and unproductive.

In her forties and just out of prison, Melissa bought a Harley-Davidson and joined a motorcycle club. Years later she told me about it, and I got to see how much her membership in that club meant to her. That was when she quit heroin, her self-proclaimed greatest life achievement. She became the motorcycle club's official photographer. She told me it was the most satisfying job she ever had (even though it paid nothing and wasn't really a "job" at all). But serving as club photographer was something she could do, a way that she could contribute to something bigger than herself. She had a deep sense of belonging to the Unknown Fools Riding Club and this sense of belonging gave her courage and support to do things she could not do alone.

There are millions of examples of people being better by joining groups. We are our best selves when we are encouraged by, or accountable to, a group. Think of all the award speeches, real and in our head, that contain the words, "I couldn't have done it without you."

My friend's story might seem extreme, but it's the same story as the grandma joining a book club or the accountant joining their professional association. It's the kid joining the sports team, the dad joining the parent-teacher association, the high school graduate joining the Marines.

As humans, not only are we naturally connected, we *want* to be connected. We want to belong. We want to be part of something bigger, deeper, and greater than ourselves. Some of us join associations, churches, and committees; some of us go to parties, concerts, and conferences; and some of us embrace a certain sports team, a rock band, a way of dressing, or a brand of beer.

Participating in the decisions of my group gives me an even deeper and more fulfilling sense of belonging. It gives me a sense that I am a part, a vital part, of something far greater than myself. I am contributing to something important. I feel that other members want me to be a member. They want me to contribute. In a good group, I don't feel the need to compete with other members of the group. We are in collaboration toward a shared higher calling.

When I am part of a good group, I gain higher aspirations. I learn from the example of others. I see what can be achieved. I get to walk a blazed trail instead of fumbling through wilderness. Not only do I get the benefit of seeing people achieve ahead of me, they cheer *me* on. I receive encouragement, support, and motivation. And I receive accountability: My fellow group members keep me honest, keep me in line, and remind me of my aspirations and how things can and will be better.

I can learn new things by reading a book or watching a video, but there's no substitute for learning in the company of others, learning together. For me, that's where the best lessons come from. When I'm part of a group, I get new knowledge and new ideas. I get to learn from experts. The best learning comes when I talk with others about what I just heard or read. The best learning comes when I try out my new ideas or new skills in front of others and get the benefit of their reaction and their support and their critique.

Real belonging comes with a sense of ownership. Here's a test. If you feel pain when your group gets hurt, that's ownership. The group is something that you are a part of. A piece of you makes up that group. The time-honored way to provide someone with a sense of ownership—no material or economic exchange required—is to invite someone into the group decisions. When I make sacrifices and actually do stuff that contributes to a group decision, I feel a sense of ownership of that decision going forward.

What if the whole world made good group decisions? What would a far more inclusive and collaborative world that look like? For one thing, there would be much more emphasis on solving shared problems and a lot less emphasis on self-advancement. There would be way more accolades for teams than for individuals.

Further, organizations would care not only about how decisions advance their own interests, but how consequences impact the interests of other groups. For instance, let's say I'm the leader of a company and I want what's best for the company's owners, employees, and customers. You could say they are my group. Yet the company also has vendors and regulators, and the company is located in a community, so they are all my group too. And the community is located in a state, in a country, in a world—more groups of which I am a part. In a better world each of us cares for the health of *all* of our groups. I know I can't please all those groups, but I can consider my impacts on them and make choices accordingly.

And in a better world, I don't just *want* what's best for my groups, I *do* what's best. My talk and my walk are aligned. I actually give things to benefit my groups, and not just in terms of what's left over after expenses and dividends. In a good group decision world, companies make real sacrifices to help their communities—all their communities. If all companies, nonprofits, and governments made truly good group decisions, everyone would be mindful of their impacts on each other. We would care deeply about income inequality, racial inequality, gender inequality, and injustice of all types. And we would cheerfully do significant stuff to help make things right.

In a world of good group decisions, no group would need to make a profit by taking from another group, but rather each group—every company, nonprofit, and government—would create new wealth from among its own people. All its people. High-functioning groups create wealth from within due to the very nature of their inclusive and collaborative processes and attitudes. In for-profit companies, this means new wealth for owners and employees. Customers benefit too—as do the communities where these companies exist. In nonprofit and government organizations, mission impact is increased and groups more effectively serve their constituents. People's lives are improved.

Organizations who make good group decisions are known for their creativity and innovation because their deliberate decision-making processes bring out the best in each person and foster collaboration among their best selves. Such organizations make leap-ahead breakthroughs. They create new knowledge and new attitudes in the world. Such organizations naturally attract people to join as employees or shareholders or members or followers or contributors or buyers. They don't need to be deceitful to get people to join. Their good decisions speak for themselves. They create something that people want to be a part of.

It's hard to imagine such a world. It's really hard. Consider how deeply ingrained the competitive values are that many of us were raised with. As a boy, I was taught to stand up for myself, no matter what. I was taught to protect my personal property. I was taught that getting more and more property was good. I was taught that it's OK to make myself feel better by making others feel worse. I was taught that it's OK to feel superior to others. I was taught that in any situation there is only one truth. I was taught that men should be in charge.

These values, every single one of them, run counter to good group decisions. I want a world with not only good group decisions but good group values. It's a world where we sacrifice self-comfort and self-advancement for advancement of the group. It's a world where, when someone does something bad, you simply make sure they are aware and help them do good. It's a world where people are not so concerned with personal property but are more concerned with common property.

In a world of good group decisions, we are focused more on giving than on getting. We know that when we give as much as we can rather than take as much as we can, our groups become stronger and we all benefit in the long run. This applies to marriages, groups of friends, companies, countries, and the group we call the human race. In a world of good group decisions, we invest in—rather than take from—our common assets such as soil, air, and water.

It's a world where people truly believe that no one of us is superior to any other of us. It's never that one person is good and another person is bad; it's always that they are just different. It's a world without fighting for singular truths—one group knowing what God wants for another group—but a world where multiple truths are peacefully tolerated. It's a world where leaders are women, where leaders collaborate rather than command, where leaders are not in charge of, but in service to, their followers.

In a world of good group decisions, there is no place for "I know what's best for you." The question, and it's always a question, is "What is best for us?" It is inviting others into a decision because you're not sure what's best. Making decisions with other people is hard, much harder than making decisions by yourself or with people you agree with. Group decision-making can be confusing, draining, and fraught with anxiety. But it doesn't have to be. I have learned over the course of my career that group decision-making can be hugely rewarding and fulfilling and fun. It can be highly productive for your group and it can bring peace and happiness to you.

"IF YOU WANT TO GO FAST, GO ALONE. IF YOU WANT TO GO FAR, GO TOGETHER."

There's an African proverb I know. I'm not sure where I learned it. I think the proverb applies to all types of groups of humans of all sizes. And I love how it give us a choice. I'm ending my book with this proverb for those two reasons, but also to remind us that the concepts in this proverb—and all the concepts in this book—are not new. They have come to us from other people far away and long ago. Yet we are all people, so the concepts apply.

"If you want to go fast, go alone. If you want to go far, go together."

INDEX

- -

downtown parking, 202
Drucker, Peter, 51
dying process, 230–31

E

Earth community, 73
Einstein, Albert, 219
elephant parables, 161–62
embarrassment, 10, 111, 189, 219
Estes, Caroline, 8–9, 120
expectations, keeping in check,
  109

F

facilitation. *See* meetings and
  facilitation
feedback, 91–92, 243–44
first thoughts, danger of sharing,
  112, 241
flat decision-making structure,
  209–10
flip charts, 224
FMC manufacturing, 49
forgiveness, 84, 101
Fox, George, 74
framing, 185–86, 191–93, 219
Fukushima Daiichi Nuclear Power
  Plant, 30

G

gap of discontent, 103–4
germination, 222–23
giving, attitude of, 67–71

breeding abundance, 70
building community, 67–68
transactional behavior vs.,
  68–69
types of giving, 68
unconditional giving, 70
without ownership, 106
without taking credit, 106
goals
aligning actions with, 143–44
analysis and revision, 190
clarity of, 152
culture, 51
defining, 141–43
focus, 229
small, 221
strategic planning, 146, 148
good in everyone, attitude of seeing, 74–78
antiracism, 75–76
decision-makers with destructive
  attitudes, 77–78
good in me, 76–77
showing respect, 74
good of the group, 125–36
disagreement with group policies, 127–31
good rules and good relationships, 131–34
reverence, 126–27
valuing everyone's gifts, 135–36
Good to Great (Collins), 144
graphic facilitators, 224
Grateful Dead, 29–30
gratitude, 103–5
choosing, 104–5
gap of discontent, 103–4

ABOUT THE AUTHOR

HERE'S WHY I'M YOUR AUTHOR—your authority
today on making good group decisions.

I'M EDUCATED BY EXPERTS.

I went to graduate school; I've done case studies on leaders making difficult decisions. I've studied the theory. I've studied a lot about how governments and governing boards work. Since leaving school, I've read a lot of books about group decision making. I've gone to a lot of conferences. I've taken a lot of training on all different aspects of group decision making. I'm a continuing learner.

I'VE WORKED FOR STATE GOVERNMENT AND FOR A NONPROFIT.

I worked for 12 years in my state capitol—some of that time for the Maine State Planning Office and some of that time for the Maine Development Foundation. I've sat through a lot of bad meetings, and I saw a lot of destructive behavior. I also sat through good meetings and experienced some exceptionally talented meeting facilitators. I've seen what works and what doesn't. I have been in the room many times with hard decisions and high stakes.

I OWN A COMPANY CALLED GOOD GROUP DECISIONS.

I have facilitated over 3,000 meetings and training sessions. Most of my clients are in the public sector: nonprofits and government agencies. I facilitate a lot of strategic planning and organizational development meetings for nonprofit boards of directors. For state government agencies, I do a lot of stakeholder and public input meetings. I have run many meetings and workshops for town and city councils, school boards, and all manner of government committees and commissions. My corporate clients tend to be small, progressive companies who want to be inclusive and collaborative. Most of my clients are women-led organizations. I generally work with the top leadership of the organizations that hire me. I have learned a great deal from my clients.

I HAVE WORKED THE POLITICAL DIVIDE.

In 2019, I won the American Award for Civic Collaboration for bringing Republicans and Democrats together to better understand each other. Having facilitated over 50 of these Make Shift Coffee Houses, as they are called, I have a good understanding of Americans' differing political values.

I LIVE IN A COHOUSING COMMUNITY.

I was involved in the start-up of the community and played a leading role in designing our consensus decision-making processes. And I have mediated a lot of conflict right here in my own neighborhood. I have lived in this community now for 25 years and so have the benefit of seeing how policies and protocols have played out. I have seen what works and what doesn't work when groups try consensus. I also chaired a private school board that made decisions by consensus.

I'M A QUAKER.

I have a spiritual life. I study and promote this stuff not just to make money but for bigger reasons. I've learned that I'm a better person when tied in tight with others: when I'm part of a group. I've learned the benefits of defining my role: what I'm responsible for and what I'm not responsible for. I believe deeply in the Quaker values of inclusion and equity: that there is that of God in every person. And my extroverted nature fits well with the Quaker value: *let your life speak.*

Yet I am not THE authority on this topic. Hundreds of books have been written about how to make decisions in groups. My book exists in the context of just one of the world's cultures and was born from just one person's experience. I've simply tried to harness the best of what I have learned over my career, organize it, and put it out there in the hopes that it will provoke you and inspire you and help you help your group make good decisions.